John George Bourinot

Local Government in Canada

An Historical Study

John George Bourinot

Local Government in Canada
An Historical Study

ISBN/EAN: 9783337188948

Printed in Europe, USA, Canada, Australia, Japan

Cover: Foto ©ninafisch / pixelio.de

More available books at **www.hansebooks.com**

JOHNS HOPKINS UNIVERSITY STUDIES

IN

HISTORICAL AND POLITICAL SCIENCE

HERBERT B. ADAMS, Editor

History is past Politics and Politics present History—*Freeman*

FIFTH SERIES

V-VI

Local Government in Canada

AN HISTORICAL STUDY

BY JOHN GEORGE BOURINOT

Clerk of the House of Commons of Canada; Honorary Secretary of the Royal Society of Canada, etc.
Author of "Parliamentary Practice and Procedure; with an Introductory Account of the Origin and Growth of Parliamentary Institutions in the Dominion of Canada," etc.

BALTIMORE

N. MURRAY, PUBLICATION AGENT, JOHNS HOPKINS UNIVERSITY

MAY and JUNE, 1887

JOHN MURPHY & CO., PRINTERS,
BALTIMORE.

TABLE OF CONTENTS.

LOCAL GOVERNMENT IN CANADA.[1]

"Local assemblies of citizens constitute the strength of free nations. Municipal institutions are to liberty what primary schools are to science; they bring it within the people's reach; they teach men how to use and how to enjoy it. A nation may establish a system of free government, but without the spirit of municipal institutions, it cannot have the spirit of liberty."—DE TOCQUEVILLE, *Democracy in America*, Vol. I. Ch. v.

I.—INTRODUCTORY.

I propose to give in this paper an historical review of the origin and growth of the municipal system of Canada. Such a review suggested itself to me after a careful perusal of the valuable series of essays that are appearing from the press of the Johns Hopkins University in the State of Maryland. These studies are remarkable for the information they give on a subject to which historians of the United States have hitherto devoted very little attention. The papers that have already been published with respect to the local institutions of Virginia, of Maryland, and of the New England States, enable us to follow step by step the progress of the people in self-government. Under the conviction that a similar paper on local government in Canada may be of some value to students of political science in the absence of any work or treatise hitherto devoted to the subject, I shall endeavor to evolve out of a chaos of old documents, statutes, and histories

[1] Read in abstract before the Royal Society of Canada, 27th May, 1886.

such facts as may give a tolerably accurate idea of the gradual development of those local institutions on which must always rest, in a great measure, the whole fabric of popular liberty.

Such a subject ought to be interesting to every Canadian, but especially to the historical student. The former may care to learn something of the history of those institutions which perform so important a part in the economy of his daily life. The latter must find a deeper attraction in tracing the origin of the municipal government of this country even to those ancient institutions, which, very many centuries ago, kept alive a spirit of liberty among our English forefathers and among the German nations.[1]

The Dominion of Canada now extends over a territory between the Atlantic and Pacific Oceans, almost equal in area to that of the United States. Its organized divisions consist of the provinces of Prince Edward Island, Nova Scotia, New Brunswick, Quebec, Ontario, Manitoba, and British Columbia, each of which possesses a very liberal system of representative government. Every province has a Lieutenant-Governor, appointed by the government of the Dominion, and a Legislature composed in Nova Scotia, New Brunswick and Quebec, of a Legislative Council nominated by the Crown, and of a Legislative Assembly elected by the people on a very liberal franchise. In Manitoba, British Columbia, and Ontario there is no Second Chamber, while in Prince Edward Island that body is elected by the people. The Northwest Territories, which extend from Manitoba to the

---

[1] "The origin of local government in England, like that of our civil liberty, must be sought in the primitive but well-ordered communities of our Saxon forefathers. . . . . The German nations, as described by Cæsar and Tacitus, were nothing but associations of self-governed villages, or larger districts, occupied by separate families, or clans, among whom there was not even the shadow of a common national allegiance, except for the purpose of war. Such was the organization of the Saxons, Jutes and Angles, when they first settled in England."—Cobden Club Essays, 1875, Local Government in England, by Hon. G. C. Brodrick, p. 3.

frontier of British Columbia—territories out of which may be formed many States as large and fertile as Minnesota—are as yet divided into mere territorial districts, over which preside a Lieutenant-Governor, appointed by the Ottawa Government, and a Council, partly nominated by the Crown, and partly elected by the people. In all of the provinces, as well as in the principal settlements, villages, and towns of the Northwest, now exists a system of municipal institutions which are the growth of the experience of the past forty years, since the people of the old provinces of Canada have grown in population and wealth, and have fully recognized the necessity of managing their purely municipal and local affairs in councils elected by themselves. These municipal institutions are the creation, and are under the jurisdiction, of the Provincial Legislatures, in accordance with the constitution, known as the British North America Act, 1867, which gives the control of all general national affairs to the Federal Government, and the administration of all local matters to the Legislatures of the provinces. As the municipal institutions of Canada, in the first instance, owe their existence to statutory enactments of the Legislatures of the provinces, so they can be amended only by the authority of the same superior bodies.

The political history of Canada may be divided into three important epochs. First of all, there was the era of the French Régime which lasted for about a century and a half, from the 3rd of July, 1608, when Champlain established his seat of government on the picturesque heights of Quebec, until 1760, when France gave up the contest with England for the supremacy on the Continent of America. Then came the period from 1760 to 1840, when the provinces slowly increased in population under British Rule, and gained valuable experience in the working of representative institutions. Then followed the important and interesting period from 1840 to 1867, when the political liberties of the people were enlarged, and they were given responsible government in the full sense of the term. Since 1867, the various provinces, united as the Dominion of Canada, have entered on a fourth era pregnant with promise.

II.—The French Régime, 1608–1760.

During the days of French domination in Canada, we look in vain for evidences of self-government in any form, such as we see in the town-meetings of Massachusetts and in the counties and parishes of Virginia, or in other local divisions of the old English colonies in America, in all of which we can see the germs of liberty and free institutions from the earliest days of their history. The system of government that was established on the banks of the St. Lawrence was the very opposite of that to which the people of New England always clung as their most valued heritage. While the townsfolk of Massachusetts were discussing affairs in town-meetings, the French inhabitants of Canada were never allowed to take part in public assemblies, but were taught to depend in the most trivial matters on a paternal government. Canada was governed as far as possible like a province of France. In the early days of the colony, when it was under the rule of mere trading companies chartered by the King, the Governors practically exercised arbitrary power, with the assistance of a Council chosen by themselves. Eventually, however, the the King, by the advice of the great Colbert, took the government of the colony into his own hands, and appointed a Governor, an Intendant, and a Supreme or Sovereign Council to administer under his own direction the affairs of the country. The Governor, who was generally a soldier, was nominally at the head of affairs, and had the direction of the defences of the colony; but to all intents and purposes, the Intendant, who was a man of legal attainments, had the greatest influence in many ways. He had the power of issuing ordinances which had the effect of law, and in the words of his commission "to order everything as he shall see just and proper." An examination of these ordinances proves conclusively the arbitrary and despotic nature of the government to which the people were subject, and the care that was taken by the authorities to give them as little liberty as possible in the management of those local matters over which the inhabitants of the British colonies exercised the fullest control. These ordinances regulated inns and markets, the building and repairs of churches and presbyteries, the construction of bridges, the maintenance of roads, and all those matters which could affect the comfort, the convenience, and the security of the community.[1]

It is interesting to notice how every effort that was made during the continuance of the French rule, to assemble the people for public purposes, and give them an opportunity of taking an interest in public questions, was systematically crushed by the orders of the government in accordance with the autocratic spirit of French monarchy. The first meeting of the inhabitants was called on the 18th of August, 1621, by Champlain, in Quebec, for the purpose of getting up a petition to the King on the affairs of Canada.[2] But this was a very exceptional event in the history of the colony. A public meeting of the parishioners to consider the cost of a new church could not be held without the special permission of the Intendant. It was the custom in the early days of the colony to hold public meetings in Quebec under the chairmanship of members of the Sovereign Council for the purpose of discussing the price and quality of bread and the supply of firewood. "Such assemblies, so controlled," says Parkman, "could scarcely, one would think, wound the tenderest susceptibilities of authority; yet there was an evident distrust of them, and after a few years this modest shred of self-government is seen no more."[3]

---

[1] "Les règlemens de police et les affaires municipales étaient aussi du domaine du gouverneur et de ses conseillers."—Doutre et Lareau, Histoire Genérale du Droit Canadien, i. 37. See also Ferland, Histoire du Canada, i. 365.

[2] Doutre et Lareau, pp. 13, 14.

[3] Parkman's Old Régime in Canada, pp. 280, 281.

We have a striking illustration of the arbitrary policy pursued toward the colony by the King and his Ministers in the action they took with reference to an attempt made by Count de Frontenac in 1672 to assemble the different orders of the colony—the clergy, the *noblesse* or *seigneurs*, the judiciary and the third estate, in imitation of the old institutions of France. He compelled the estates of Canada, as he called them, to take the new oath of allegiance before a great assemblage of persons. The French King did not long leave the haughty Governor in doubt as to his opinion of this innovation on the policy laid down for the government of the colony. "The assembling and division that you have made," wrote Colbert, "of all the inhabitants of the country into three orders or estates with the object of administering to them the oath of allegiance might have some effect for the moment; but it is well to consider that you should always observe in the administration of public affairs those forms which are followed here and that our kings have deemed it inexpedient for a long time past to assemble the States-General of their kingdom, with the view perhaps of destroying the ancient system. Under these circumstances you should very rarely, and in fact it would be better if you should never, give this form to the people of the country. It will be advisable, even after a while, when the colony is more vigorous than at present, to suppress by degrees the syndic who presents petitions in the name of the inhabitants, as it seems better that everyone should speak for himself, and no one for all."[1]

The history of the officer just named, the syndic, of itself gives us some striking evidence of the stern determination of the government to stamp out every vestige of popular institutions, however insignificant it might be. The *syndics d'habitations* are said to have been originally constituted by Colbert to act as municipal officers appointed by the people of the

---

[1] Doutre et Lareau, pp. 169, 170; Chauveau, Notice sur la publication des Régistres du Conseil Souverain, etc., p. 34.

cities to preserve public rights. The references to these functionaries in the history of those times are very vague: they appear to have existed in Quebec, Montreal, and Three Rivers in 1647, but they ceased to exist by 1661. The government was determined to have no town-meetings or municipal officers in the province of Quebec. In 1663, a meeting of the citizens of Quebec was called by the Supreme Council, on the requisition of the Attorney-General, to elect a Mayor and two Aldermen for that town. The people accordingly chose Jean-Baptiste Legardeur, Sieur de Repentigny, for Mayor, and Jean Madry and Claude Charron for Aldermen; but these persons soon resigned in consequence, it is well understood, of the influence brought to bear upon them by the authorities. They declared that, having regard to the smallness of the population, it would be better to appoint a syndic. The first election held for this purpose was annulled, and another, called irregularly by the Governor, made a nomination. It appears that the Bishop, Monseigneur de Laval, a haughty, determined man, who proved himself during his memorable career in Canada a true descendant of the great house of Montmorency, was opposed to the action taken in this matter, and his friends in the council protested against the swearing in and installation of the syndic. The Governor, M. de Mezy, took upon himself to suspend the obstinate councillors, and consequently committed a violation of the royal instructions, for he had no power of appointing these functionaries without the consent of the Bishop, or of dismissing or suspending them at his own discretion.[1] Without dwelling further on these official squabbles, frequent enough in those times, it is only necessary to add that the sequel was that the country heard no more of attempts to establish even a semblance of popular representative government in the towns of Canada. The policy of the King and his advisers was determinately antagonistic to such

---

[1] Chauveau, pp. 24–30; Garneau, i. 179, 180; Parkman's Old Régime, p. 281; Doutre et Lareau, p. 129.

institutions. "It is of great consequence," wrote Meules to the minister in 1685, "not to give any liberty to the people to express their opinions."[1]

The administration of local affairs was exclusively under the control of the King's officers at Quebec. As I have already shown, the ordinances of the Intendant and of the Council were the law. The local or territorial divisions of the colony had no connection, as did the townships, parishes, and counties of the English colonies in America, with the local affairs of the people. The country was subdivided into the following divisions for purposes of government, settlement, and justice:[2]

1. Districts.
2. Seigniories.
3. Parishes.

The districts were simply established for judicial and legal purposes, and each of them bore the name of the principal town within its limits, viz: Quebec, also called the *Prévôté de Québec*, Montreal, and Three Rivers. In each of these districts there was a judge, appointed by the King, to adjudicate on all civil and criminal matters. An appeal was allowed in the most trivial cases to the Supreme or Superior Council, which also exercised original jurisdiction.[3]

The greater part of Canada was divided into large estates or seigniories, which were held under a modified system of feudal tenure, established by Richelieu in 1627,[4] with the view of creating a colonial aristocracy or *noblesse*, and of stimulating settlement in a wilderness. By this system, which lasted until 1854,[5] lands were as a rule held immediately from the King

---

[1] Meules au Ministre, 1685.

[2] Bouchette, A Topographical Description of the Province of Lower Canada, etc., pp. 86, 87.

[3] Doutre et Lareau, p. 130.

[4] Garneau, i. 171.

[5] It was abolished after many years of agitation by 18 Vict., c. 3.

en fief or *en roture.* The seignior, on his accession to the estate, was required to pay homage to the King, or to his feudal superior in case the lands were granted by another than the King.[1] The seignior received his land gratuitously from the crown, and granted them to his vassals who were generally known as *habitants* or cultivators of the soil. The *habitant* or *censitaire* held his property by the tenure of *en censive*, on condition of making annual payments in money or produce known as *cens et rente*, which were ridiculously small in the early times of the colony.[2] He was obliged to grind his corn at the seignior's mill (*moulin banal*[3]), bake his bread in the seignior's oven, give his lord a tithe of the fish caught in his waters, and comply with other conditions at no time onerous or strictly enforced in the days of the French regime. The land of the *censitaire* went to his heirs, but in case he sold it during his lifetime, one-twelfth of the purchase money was given under the name of *lods et ventes* to the seignior. In case the latter at any time transferred, by sale or otherwise, his seigniory—except of course in the event of natural hereditary succession—he had to pay a *quint* or fifth part of the whole purchase money to his feudal superior, but he was allowed a reduction (*rabat*) of two-thirds when the money was paid down immediately.[4]

The system, irreconcilable as it is with our modern ideas of free settlement, had some advantages in a new country like

---

[1] Parkman, p. 245.

[2] Half a *sou*, and half a pint of wheat, or a few live capons, wheat, and eggs, would represent the *cens et rente* for each arpent in early days. Parkman's Old Régime, p. 249.

[3] The government appear to have rigidly enforced the seignior's rights in the case of the *moulin banal.* For instance, in 1706, the Intendant issued an ordinance forbidding the Dame de La Forêt from turning her mill in the county of St. Laurent while there was a *moulin banal* in that place. Doutre et Lareau, p. 237.

[4] For a succinct description of the main features of the seigniorial tenure, see Parkman's Old Régime, ch. 15; Garneau, i. 171–174.

Canada, where the government managed everything and colonization was not left to chance. The seignior was obliged to cultivate his estate at the risk of forfeiture—and many estates were from time to time resumed by the crown—and consequently it was absolutely necessary that he should exert himself to bring settlers upon his lands. The conditions of the tenure were in early times so trivial as not to burden the settler. The obligation of the *censitaire* to grind his corn in the seignior's mill was an advantage, since it insured him the means of procuring bread, which it would have been otherwise difficult to find in a country where there was neither money nor enterprise. The seigniories were practically so many territorial divisions where the *seigneur* was master and adviser to his *censitaires.* He had the right of dispensing justice in certain cases, though this was a right he very rarely exercised.[1] As respects civil affairs, however, both lord and vassal were to all intents and purposes on the same footing, for they were equally ignored in matters of government.

In the days of the French régime, the only towns for many years were Quebec, Montreal, and Three Rivers. Villages were but slow in growth, despite the efforts of the government to encourage them. In remote and exposed places—like those on the Richelieu, where officers and soldiers of the Carignan regiment had been induced to settle—palisaded villages had been built; but in the rural parts of the province generally, the people appear to have considered their own convenience. The principal settlements were, in the course of time, established on the banks of the St. Lawrence from Quebec to Montreal. The people chose the banks of the river, as affording them in those days the easiest means of intercommunication. As the lots of a grant *en censive* were limited in area—four arpents in front by forty in depth—the farms in the course of

[1] The seigniors rarely exercised their judicial rights; the Seminary of St. Sulpice was almost the only one to do so; the Council exercised superior jurisdiction in all cases. Doutre et Lareau, pp. 133, 305.

time assumed the appearance of a continuous settlement on the river. These various settlements became known in local phraseology as *Côtes*, apparently from their natural situation on the banks of the river. This is the derivation of Côte des Neiges, Côte St. Louis, Côte St. Paul, and of many picturesque villages in the neighborhood of Montreal and Quebec.[1]

The parishes were established for ecclesiastical purposes, and were grouped on each side of the St. Lawrence and Richelieu. Their extent was exactly defined in September, 1721, by a regulation made by Messieurs de Vaudreuil and Begon, assisted by the Bishop of Quebec, and confirmed by an *Arrêt du Conseil* of the 2nd of March, 1722.[2] These parishes are constantly referred to in the ordinances of the Superior Council, in connection with the administration of local affairs. In the parishes, the influential men were the *Curé*, the seignior, and the captain of the militia.[3] The seignior, from his social position, exercised a considerable weight in the community, but not to the degree that the representative of the Church enjoyed. From the earliest time in the history of the colony, we find the Roman Catholic Church exercising a dominant influence—an influence, it must be admitted, discreetly and wisely used for the welfare of the people committed to its spiritual care.

---

[1] Parkman's Old Régime, p. 234.

[2] Edits et Ordonnances, i. 443. Doutre et Lareau, pp. 259, 260. Bouchette's Canada, p. 86.

[3] "The most important persons in a parish were the curé, the seignior, and the militia captain. The seignior had his bench of honor in the church. Immediately behind it was the bench of the militia captain, whose duty it was to drill the able-bodied men of the neighborhood. . . . Next in honor came the local judge, if any there was, and the church wardens." Parkman's Old Régime, p. 387. The precedence in church and processions was regulated by ordinance. See Doutre et Lareau, p. 242.

[4] "Lower Canada had, when we received it at the conquest, two institutions which alone preserved the semblance of order and civilization in the community—the Catholic Church and the militia, which was so constituted and used as partially to supply the want of better civil institutions."—Lord Durham's Report, p. 31.

Next to the curé in importance was the captain of militia, who was exceedingly useful in the absence of civil authorities in carrying out the orders and instructions of the Government in the parishes. The whole province was formed into a militia district so that, in times of war, the inhabitants might be obliged to perform military service under the French Governor. In times of peace, these militia officers executed the orders of the Governor and Intendant in all matters affecting the King. A captain was appointed for each parish, and in some of the larger divisions there were two or three.[1]

By reference to the numerous ordinances of the Intendant, we can see pretty accurately how such local matters as the construction, maintenance and repair of roads and bridges were managed in the seigniories and parishes. In case it was considered necessary to build a church or presbytery, the Intendant authorized the *habitants* to assemble for the purpose of choosing from among themselves four persons to make, with the curé, the seignior, and the captain of the militia, an estimate of the expense of the structure. It was the special care of the captain of the militia to look after the work, and see that each parishioner did his full share.[2] It was only in church matters, in fact, that the people of a parish had a voice, and even in these, as we see, they did not take the initiative. The Quebec authorities must in all such cases first issue an ordinance.

All the roads and bridges of the colony were under the supervision of the *grand voyer*, or superintendent of highways, appointed by the King. We find in the proceedings of the Council on the 1st of February, 1706, the regulations which governed this important officer in the discharge of his duties. He was obliged to visit all the seigniories at certain times of the year and make provision for the highways wherever necessary. The roads and other local improvements were con-

---

[1] Doutre et Lareau, p. 136.

[2] Edits et ordonnances, ii. 295.

structed after consultation with the proprietors of lands and the most responsible persons of the place, at the expense of the people immediately interested. All the work was performed under the direction of the captain of militia in the parish.[1]

The position of the people in French Canada for a century and a half has been tersely set forth by the writers to whom we have frequently referred : "Without education, without an opportunity of taking part in public affairs, without an interest in the public offices, all of which were filled up by persons sent out by the Government, the Canadian people were obliged to seek, in the clearing of the forest, in the cultivation of the field, in the chase and in adventure, the means of livelihood, and hardly ever busied themselves with public matters. Sometimes they thought they were becoming 'a people' on this continent, and might acquire a larger degree of liberty, but all such aspirations were promptly checked by the governor, the intendant and the bishop, in obedience to the instructions of the King. No social union existed between the people, no guarantees for civil liberty were ever established. On every occasion the people were taught to have no ambition for civil power, or for a share in public business. Reduced at last to a state of passive obedience, they accepted the orders and edicts of the King without a murmur."[2]

It is easy to understand that the result of this autocratic, illiberal system of government was complete social and political stagnation.[3] It was not until the people of French Canada

---

[1] Edits et ordonnances, ii. 135.

[2] Doutre et Lareau, p. 308.

[3] "The institutions of France, during the period of the colonization of Canada were, perhaps, more than those of any other European nation, calculated to repress the intelligence and freedom of the great mass of the people. These institutions followed the Canadian colonist across the Atlantic. The same central, ill-organized, unimproving and repressive despotism extended over him. Not merely was he allowed no voice in the government of the province, or the choice of his rulers, but he was not even permitted to associate with his neighbors for the regulation of those municipal affairs which the central authority neglected under the pretext of managing." Lord Durham's Report, p. 9.

had been for many years under a British system of government, that they awoke to the full consciousness of their rights, and began to take that practical interest in public affairs which was the best evidence of their increased intelligence.

III.—Lower Canada, 1760–1840.

For three years after the conquest of Canada, the government was in the hands of military chiefs who had their headquarters at Quebec, Montreal, and Three Rivers, the *chefs lieux* of the three departments into which General Amherst, the first English Governor-General, divided the new province. During this military régime the people as a rule settled their difficulties among themselves, and did not resort to the military tribunals which were established to administer law throughout the conquered territory.[1] In 1763, King George III. established four new governments in America, viz.: Quebec, East Florida, West Florida, and Grenada. For nearly thirty years, the people of the government of Quebec were not represented in a Legislature, but were governed up to 1774 by a Governor-General, and an Executive Council, composed in the first instance, of the two Lieutenant-Governors of Montreal and Three Rivers, of the Surveyor-General of Customs, and of eight others chosen from the leading residents of the province.[2] In 1774 the Imperial Parliament for the first time intervened in the affairs of the country, and passed the Quebec Act, by which the government was entrusted to a Governor-General and a Legislative Council appointed by the Crown, inasmuch as it was deemed "inexpedient to call an Assembly." This irresponsible body was to contain not more than twenty-three and not less than seventeen members, and had power with the consent of the Governor-General "to make ordinances for the

---

[1] Attorney-General Thurlow's Report in Christie's History of Lower Canada, i. 49, 50.

[2] Christie, i. 49, 50.

peace, welfare, and good government of the province." It had no authority, however, to impose any taxes or duties, except such as the inhabitants of any town or district might be authorized to assess or levy within its precincts for the purpose of making roads, erecting and repairing public buildings, or for any other purpose respecting the local convenience and economy of such town or district.[1]

During the military régime, the captains of militia dispensed justice and carried out the orders of the authorities in the parishes.[2] The King, in 1763, gave instructions to Governor Murray, who succeeded General Amherst, to lay out townships and provide town sites, with the view of encouraging the settlement of English-speaking people. Provision was also made for building a church, and for giving 400 acres of land to the support of a clergyman, and 200 acres for a schoolmaster.[3] In 1764 the Governor established Courts of Quarter-Sessions for the trial of petty causes. These Courts were composed of Justices of the Peace, who had to address their warrants to the captains and other officers of militia in the first instance.[4] The majority of the inhabitants dwelling in each parish were also permitted to elect, on the 24th of June in each year, six men to act as *Baillis* and *Sous-Baillis*.[5] The names of these men were sent in to the Deputy Secretary of the province, and the Governor-General, with the consent of the Council, appointed the persons who were to act. These officers had for some years the inspection of the highways and bridges, and also acted as constables. In 1777, it was deemed advisable to pass an ordinance providing for the repair and maintenance of the roads and bridges in the province, under the direction of the *Grand Voyer*, whose office was reëstablished

[1] 14 Geo. III. c. 83; Bourinot's Parliamentary Procedure, ch. i. on Parliamentary Institutions in Canada, pp. 9–12.

[2] Doutre et Lareau, p. 485.

[3] *Ibid.*, p. 563.

[4] *Ibid.*, p. 589.

[5] *Ibid.*, p. 590.

in accordance with the desire of the Imperial Government to continue the old institutions of the country, to which the people were accustomed. The old French system was practically again in force. The proprietors and farmers were required to keep up the roads and bridges that passed by their respective properties. All repairs were performed by statute labor or at the cost of the parish. The Judges of Common Pleas on Circuit were to report on the state of the communications, as provided for in the ordinance.[1]

In 1791, a very important constitutional change took place in the political condition of Canada. At the close of the American War of Independence, a large number of people known as United Empire Loyalists, on account of their having remained faithful to the British Crown during that great struggle, came and settled in the provinces. Some ten thousand persons, at least, made their homes in Upper Canada, while a considerable number found their way to the Eastern Townships which lie to the south of the St. Lawrence, between the Montreal district and the frontier of the United States. The Parliament of Great Britain then thought it advisable to separate the French and English nationalities by forming the two provinces on the St. Lawrence and the Great Lakes, known until 1867 as Lower Canada and Upper Canada. To the people of both sections were granted representative institutions.[2] By a proclamation of the Governor-General, dated 7th of May, 1792, Lower Canada was divided, for legislative purposes, into the following twenty-one counties:—Bedford, Buckingham, Cornwallis, Devon, Dorchester, Effingham, Gaspé, Hampshire, Hertford, Huntingdon, Kent, Leinster, Montreal, St. Maurice, Northumberland, Orleans, Quebec, Richelieu, Surrey, Warwick, and York.[3] The names of some

---

[1] Ordinances for the Province of Quebec (Brown and Gilmore), p. 86.

[2] 31 Geo. III. c. 31; Bourinot, p. 14.

[3] Bouchette's Topographical Description of Lower Canada, etc., p. 86. It appears that Nova Scotia was the first province in British North America to establish the old Norman division of "County," which is the equivalent of the Saxon "Shire." See *infra*, p. 44.

of these divisions recall well-known counties or shires in England.

The system of government established in 1791 continued in force until the suspension of the constitution of Lower Canada, as a consequence of the rebellion of 1837–8, under the leadership of Papineau and other men whose names are familiar to all students of Canadian political history. During these years, the country was practically governed by the Governor-General and the Executive and Legislative Councils, both nominated by the former. The popular house, however, had little influence or power as long as the Government was not responsible to the people's representatives, and was indifferent to their approbation or support. The result was an irrepressible conflict between the Assembly, and the Legislative and Executive Councils supported by the Governor-General. The fact was, the whole system of government was based on unsound principles. The representative system, granted to the people, did not go far enough, since it should have given the people full control over the public revenues and the administration of public affairs, in accordance with the principles of ministerial responsibility to Parliament as understood in the parent state. More than that, it failed because it had not been established at the outset on a basis of local self-government, as was the case in the United States, where the institutions of New England and other colonies had gradually prepared the people for a free system of government. Turning to the remarkable report on the affairs of Canada which bears the name of Lord Durham,[1] who was Governor-General and High Commissioner in 1839, we find the following clear appreciation of the weakness of the system in operation for so many years in the old provinces of

[1] This remarkable document, it is now well understood, was written by Mr. Charles Buller, who accompanied Lord Durham in the capacity of secretary. "In fact written by Mr. Charles Buller, and embodying the opinions of Mr. Gibbon Wakefield and Sir William Molesworth on Colonial policy."—Note by Mr. Reeve to Greville's Memoirs (second part), i. 142.

Canada: "If the wise example of those countries in which a free and representative government has alone worked well had been in all respects followed in Lower Canada, care would have been taken that at the same time that a parliamentary system, based on a very extended suffrage, was introduced into the country, the people should have been entrusted with a complete control over their own local affairs, and been trained for taking their part in the concerns of the province by their experience in the management of that local business which was most interesting and most easily intelligible to them. But the inhabitants of Lower Canada were unhappily initiated into self-government at the wrong end, and those who were not trusted with the management of a parish were enabled by their votes to influence the destinies of a State."[1]

The following divisions existed in Lower Canada, between 1792 and 1840, none of which, however, were constituted with a view to purposes of local government:—

1. Districts.
2. Counties.
3. Parishes.
4. Townships.

The four districts were Quebec, Three Rivers, Montreal, and St. Francis, which were established for purely judicial purposes. The courts therein had unlimited and supreme original jurisdiction. In addition to these superior districts there was the inferior division of Gaspé with a limited jurisdiction.

The counties were, as I have already intimated, established for parliamentary objects; for Lord Durham observed that he knew "of no purpose for which they were constituted, except for the election of members for the House of Assembly."[2] The parishes, into which the seigniories were divided, were

[1] Lord Durham's Report, p. 35.

[2] Report, p. 35.

the old divisions established in the days of the French régime. The limits of the parishes, as set forth in the ordinance of 1721, were not strictly adhered to as the population spread, and settlements became more numerous. It was consequently found necessary from time to time to build many new churches, that the means and accommodation for religious worship might keep pace with the numerical increase of the congregations. For the support of these churches, portions of ancient parishes were, as the occasion arose, constituted into new ones.[1] The townships were established a few years after the conquest, principally for surveying purposes, in order to meet the requirements of the considerable English population that in the course of time flowed into Upper and Lower Canada.[2]

The people that dwelt in the local divisions had no power to assess themselves for local improvements, but whenever a road or bridge was wanted it was necessary to apply to the Legislature. In consequence of this, the time of that body was constantly occupied with the consideration of measures, which should have been the work of such local councils as existed in different parts of the United States. The little schemes and intrigues into which the representatives of different localities entered in order to promote and carry some local work and make themselves popular with their constituents gave rise to a great deal of what is known, in American parlance, as "log-rolling." "When we want a bridge, we take a judge to build it" was the forcible way, according to Lord Durham's Report,[3] in which a member of the provincial Legislature described the tendency in those days to retrench on the most important departments of the public service in order to satisfy the pressing demands for local works.

It would be supposed that the British-speaking people of the townships, whose early lives had been passed in the midst

---

[1] Bouchette, p. 86.

[2] Bouchette, p. 87; Lord Durham's Report, p. 36.

[3] Report, p. 29.

of the liberal local institutions of the old British Colonies, would have been desirous of introducing into their respective districts at least a semblance of municipal government. We look in vain, however, for such an effort on their part. They appear to have quietly acquiesced in a state of things calculated to repress a spirit of local enterprise and diminish the influence of the people in the administration of public affairs. Indeed, we have some evidence that the government itself was prepared for many years to discourage every attempt to introduce into Canada anything like the local system that had so long existed in New England. British statesmen probably remembered the strong influence that the town-meetings of Boston had in encouraging a spirit of rebellion, and thought it advisable to stifle at the outset any aspirations that the Canadian colonists might have in the direction of such doubtful institutions. "I understand," wrote Mr. Richards in a report to the Secretary of State for the colonies, ordered by the House of Commons to be printed as late as March, 1832, "that the Vermonters had crossed the line and had partially occupied several townships, bringing with them their municipal institutions; and that when the impropriety of electing their own officers was pointed out to them, they had quietly given them up, and promised to conform to those of Canada."[1]

While the Legislature was, to all intents and purposes, a large municipal council for the initiation and supervision of all local improvements, the affairs of the different parishes and townships were administered as far as consonant with the old French system. The *Grand Voyer* and Militia Captain continued to be important functionaries in the administration of local affairs. All the highways and bridges had to be repaired and maintained under the direction of the *Grand Voyer* or his deputy. Whenever it was necessary to open a new road or to change an old one, it was the duty of these officials, on receiving a petition from the locality, to call a

---

[1] Lord Durham's Report, p. 36.

public meeting with reference to the matter, by a notice published at the parish church door after the morning service. The *Grand Voyer* or his deputy had the power of dividing every parish, seigniory, or township, into such sections as he should think proper, and allot to each an overseer of highways and bridges, to be chosen at a meeting of householders, called and presided over by the eldest captain or senior officer of militia. These meetings were held in the public room of the parsonage of the parish, or at such other place as the captain of the militia might direct. The *Grand Voyer* had alone the power of appointing a surveyor of roads and of considering and deciding on reports made by such officers to him on the subject of highways. It was the duty of the Justices of the Peace, assembled in quarter sessions, to hear and adjudicate on all questions that might arise under this law. The same regulations, however, did not apply to the cities and parishes of Quebec and Montreal. Here the Justices of the Peace in sessions had practically the regulation of highways, streets, and local improvements, and appointed all the officers necessary to carry out the same. They also fixed and determined the sums of money that had to be paid for such purposes.[1]

As a matter of fact, the *Grands Voyers*, who lived in Quebec, Montreal, and Three Rivers, had no very onerous functions to discharge. The people of the parishes and townships learned to depend on the Legislature and only performed the work imposed on them by the law regulating statute labor. The absence of effective municipal institutions was particularly conspicuous in the cities of Quebec and Montreal, where it would be expected that more public spirit would be shown. "These cities," I again quote from Lord Durham's Report,[2] "were incorporated a few years ago by a temporary provincial Act of which the renewal was rejected in 1836. Since that time these cities have been without any municipal government

[1] See Lower Canada Statutes, 1796.

[2] Report, p. 36.

and the disgraceful state of the streets and the utter absence of lighting are consequences which arrest the attention of all and seriously affect the comfort and security of the inhabitants."

In every matter affecting the administration of civil and judicial affairs there appears to have been a remarkable absence of anything approaching a workable system by which the people might manage their affairs. More than that, there was actually an insufficiency of public officers for the administration of justice. Outside the cities, the machinery of civil government was singularly defective. A Sheriff was appointed only for each of the four judicial districts. Neither Sheriffs nor Constables nor parochial officers could be found in the majority of the counties of the province. It is true there were a number of Justices of the Peace who assembled in Quarter-Sessions in accordance with the system so long in vogue in England and her colonies, but these men were appointed without much regard to their qualifications for the position, and even the permanent salaried Chairmen, appointed by the Crown, were in the course of time abolished by the Legislature, and these inferior Courts consequently deprived of the services of men generally of superior attainments.[1] Practically, the affairs of each parish were regulated by the Curé, the Seignior and the Captain of militia, as in the days of French government. Thanks to the influence of these men, peace and order prevailed. Indeed as we review the history of French Canada in all times, we cannot pay too high a tribute to the usefulness of the French Canadian clergy in the absence of the settled institutions of local government. In fact, it was only in ecclesiastical affairs that the people ever had an opportunity of exercising a certain influence. The old institution of the *fabrique*—which still exists[2] in all its vigor

[1] Lord Durham's Report, p. 39.

[2] The law still makes special provision for the erection and division of parishes, the construction and repair of churches, parsonages, cemeteries, and for the meeting of fabriques. Every decree for the canonical erection of a new parish, or for the subdivision, dismemberment or union of any parishes,

—enabled them to meet together whenever it was necessary to repair a church or presbytery. When the religious services were over, the people assembled at the church door and discussed their affairs.

No doubt the influences of the old French Régime prevailed in Lower Canada for a long while after the conquest. A people whose ancestors had never learned the advantages of local self-government, would be naturally slow to awake to the necessity of adopting institutions under which the American colonists had flourished. It may be true, as Mr. Parkman says, that the French colonists, when first brought to America, could not have suddenly adopted the political institutions to which the English-speaking colonists at once had recourse as the natural heritage of an English race. It is certainly true, as the eminent American historian adds, that the mistake of the rulers of New France "was not that they exercised authority, but that they exercised too much of it, and instead of weaning the child to go alone kept him in perpetual leading strings, making him, if possible, more and more dependent, and less and less fit for freedom." When the French Canadian became subject to the British Crown, he was, literally, a child who had never been taught to think for himself in public affairs. He was perfectly unskilled in matters appertaining to self-government, and had no comprehension whatever of that spirit of self-reliance and free action which characterizes the peoples brought up under Teutonic and English institutions. In the course of time, however, the best minds among them began to appreciate fully the advantages of free government, and to their struggles for the extension of representative gov-

---

or with regard to the boundaries of parishes, must be publicly read from the pulpit or chapel of the parish, and other formal steps taken to notify the inhabitants of the proposed measure, before Commissioners appointed by the State can give civil recognition to the decree. On the *procès verbal* of these officers, the Lieutenant-Governor may issue a proclamation under the great seal of the province, erecting such parish for civil purposes. See Consol. Stat. Low. Can., c. 18, and amending Statutes.

ernment the people of British North America owe a debt of gratitude. It took a long while, however, to educate the people of French Canada up to the necessity of establishing a liberal system of municipal institutions. As we shall see, before the close of this paper, it was not until after the Union of 1840, that the French Canadians could be brought to acknowledge the benefits of local taxation imposed by their own local representatives. In this respect, they made less progress than the people of Upper Canada, to whose history we shall now proceed to refer.

IV.—Upper Canada, 1792–1840.

As I have already stated, Upper Canada was settled by United Empire Loyalists, who came into the country after the War of Independence. The majority of these people settled on the shores of Lake Ontario, in the vicinity of Kingston and the Bay of Quinté, in the Niagara district, and in other favored localities by Lakes Ontario and Erie.[1] On the 24th of July, 1788, the Governor-General issued a proclamation[2] constituting the following districts in Western or Upper Canada, viz., Luneburg, Mecklenburg, Nassau, Hesse.

Luneburg comprised the towns or tracts known by the names of Lancaster, Charlottenburg, Cornwall, Osnabruck, Williamsburg, Matilda, Edwardsburg, Augusta, and Elizabethtown. Mecklenburg comprised Pittsburg, Kingston, Ernestown, Fredericksburg, Adolphustown, Marysburg, Sophiasburg, Ameliasburg, Sydney, Thurlow, Richmond, and Camden. Nassau comprised the extensive district which extends from Trent to Long Point on Lake Erie, and Hesse,

---

[1] Ryerson's Loyalists in America, ii. 189.

[2] See Proclamation in Collection of Acts and Ordinances relating to Upper Canada, York, 1818. Luneburg is correctly spelt in the Proclamation, but in course of time it became, for some unexplained reason, "Lunenburg." The name still survives in the changed form in Nova Scotia.

the rest of the western part of Canada to Lake St. Clair.[1] To each of these districts were appointed a Judge and a Sheriff, and justice was administered in Courts of Common Pleas. The Justices were taken from the best men the country offered in the absence of persons of legal attainments.[2] The Judges in those primitive times seem to have possessed almost absolute power.

The first local divisions of Upper Canada appear to have been the townships. The British Government was extremely liberal in its grants of land to the Loyalists and the officers and soldiers who settled in Upper Canada and the other provinces. The grants were made free of expense on the following scale: to a field officer, 5,000 acres; to a captain, 3,000; to a subaltern, 2,000; to a private, 200. Surveys were first made of the lands extending from Lake St. Francis, on the St. Lawrence, to beyond the Bay of Quinté. Townships were laid out and divided into concessions and lots of 200 acres. Each township generally extended nine miles in front and twelve in the rear, and varied from 80,000 to 40,000 acres. The townships were not named for many years, but were numbered in two divisions.[3] One division embraced the townships below Kingston on the St. Lawrence, and the other townships westward to the head of the Bay of Quinté. One of the first set-

---

[1] Canniff's History of the Settlement of Upper Canada, p. 62; also foregoing Proclamation.

[2] Judge Duncan of Luneburg was a storekeeper and a Captain in the militia; he dealt out law, dry goods, and groceries alternately. *Ibid.*, p. 506.

[3] Canniff; Ryerson, ii. 224–5. Dr. Scadding, Toronto of Old, p. 362, gives an amusing account of the frivolous way in which many of the old townships of Upper Canada were named in the course of years. Flos, Tay and Tiny, which are names of three now populous townships in the Penetanguishene district, are a commemoration of three of Lady Sarah Maitland's lapdogs. Some one wrote *Jus et Norma*, as a joke, across a plan of a newly surveyed region, and three townships were consequently known as "Jus," "Et," and "Norma" for years until they were changed to Barrie, Palmerston and Clarendon respectively. "Aye," "Yea," and "No" were also designations of local divisions.

tlers of Upper Canada has given us the following description of the mode in which the townships were granted by the government:—

"At length the time came in July, for the townships to be given out. The Governor came and having assembled the companies before him, called for Mr. Grass, and said: 'Now you were the first person to mention this fine country, and have been here formerly as a prisoner of war. You must have the first choice. The townships are numbered, first, second, third, fourth and fifth; which do you choose?' 'The first township' (Kingston). Then the Governor says to Sir John Johnson, 'Which do you choose?' He replies, 'The second township' (Ernestown). To Colonel Rogers, 'Which do you choose?' He says, 'The third' (Fredericksburg). To Major Vanalstine, 'Which do you choose,' 'The Fourth' (Adolphustown). Then Colonel McDonell got the fifth township (Marysburg). So, after this manner, the first settlement of Loyalists in Upper Canada was made."[1]

The districts which were constituted in 1788 were intended mainly for judicial purposes, and were named after great houses in Germany, allied to the royal family of England. The same was the case with the first townships that were laid out. The first township was called Kingstown, after His Majesty George III; Ernestown after Ernest Augustus, eighth child of the King; Adolphustown, after another son.[2] Provision was made for future towns during the first surveys. A plot was generally reserved in some locality which seemed especially adapted for a town. This was the case in Adolphustown, where a lot was granted to each of the settlers. But

---

[1] Ryerson, ii. 209.

[2] "King George III, who died in 1820, aged 82, having reigned 60 years, had a family of 15 children, whose names were George, Frederick, William Henry, Charlotte Augusta, Matilda, Edward, Sophia Augusta, Elizabeth, Ernest Augustus, Augustus Frederick, Adolphus Frederick, Mary Sophia, Octavius, Alfred, and Amelia. These royal names were appropriated to the townships, towns, and districts." Canniff, p. 439.

towns were of very slow growth, until some years after the establishment of a separate government in Upper Canada, when settlers began to flow steadily into a country whose fertility and productiveness commenced at last to be understood. Not a few of the towns owe their establishment to private enterprise and prescience in the first instance.[1]

In 1791 Upper Canada was separated from French Canada, and became a province with a Legislature composed of a Lieutenant-Governor, a Legislative Council appointed by the Crown, and a Legislative Assembly elected by the people.[2] When Lieutenant-Governor Simcoe undertook the administration of the affairs of the new province, he issued a proclamation dividing it into nineteen counties, as follows: Glengary, Stormont, Dundas, Grenville, Leeds, Frontenac, Ontario, Addington, Lenox, Prince Edward, Hastings, Northumberland, Durham, York, Lincoln, Norfolk, Suffolk, Essex, and Kent.[3] Some of the well-settled counties were divided into ridings,[4] each of which sent a representative to the Legislature. In other cases one representative was elected for two or more counties. One of the first Acts of the Legislature was to change the names of the four divisions established in 1788 to the Eastern, Midland, Home, and Western Districts.[5] In the

---

[1] "Windsor (now Whitby) was so named about 1819 by its projector, Mr. John Scadding, the original grantee of a thousand acres in this locality. On a natural harbor of Lake Ontario, popularly know as Big Bay, Mr. Scadding laid out the town, built the first house, and named the streets, three of them after his three sons—John, Charles, and Henry." Ryerson, ii. 260. One of these sons, here mentioned, is the well-known antiquarian of Toronto, Rev. Dr. Scadding.

[2] 31 Geo. III, c. 31.

[3] See Proclamation in Statutes of Upper Canada, i. 23.

[4] Trithings or ridings were divisions peculiar to Yorkshire and Lincolnshire, though Robertson (Scotland under her early Kings, iii. 433) is inclined to trace them in Kent and Surrey. Bishop Stubbs, however, (Constitutional History, i. 100) considers the view "very interesting but very conjectural."

[5] Upp. Can. Stat. 32 Geo. III, c. 8.

course of years the number was increased by the addition of the Johnstown, Newcastle, Niagara, London, and Gore Districts.[1] These districts were intended mainly for legal and judicial purposes. But all these old names, so familiar in provincial history, have become obliterated by the county organizations.

The Duke de la Rochefoucault-Liancourt, who visited the country in 1795, and had several interviews with Governor Simcoe, at Newark, now Niagara, the old capital of Upper Canada, informs us that the division of the four districts into counties was "purely military, and related merely to the enlisting, completing and assembling of the militia. The militia of each county is commanded by a lieutenant."[2] Whilst the Duke was, no doubt, correct in the main, it must not be forgotten that the erection of counties was also necessary for purposes of representation. A section of the act establishing the Constitution of Upper Canada expressly provided: His Majesty may authorize "the Governor or Lieutenant-Governor of each of the provinces of Upper and Lower Canada to issue a proclamation dividing such province into districts or counties or circles, towns and townships, and appointing the limits thereof, and declaring and appointing the number of representatives to be chosen by each of such districts, counties or circles, towns and townships respectively."[3] Members for the Legislature were then, and for many years afterward, chosen by freeholders having real property to the yearly value of forty shillings in districts, counties or circles, and five pounds sterling in towns and townships, or who paid a rental in the latter at the rate of ten pounds sterling a year.[4]

The Legislature was composed of plain, practical men, who went energetically to work in the first sessions to provide for the wants of the few thousands of people scattered through-

---

[1] Bouchette, p. 590. Scadding's Toronto, p. 361.

[2] De la Rochefoucault-Liancourt, Voyage dans les États-Unis et le Haut Canada, i. 434.

[3] 31 Geo. III, c. 31. s. 14.

[4] Imp. Stat. 31 Geo. III, c. 31.

out the wide extent of country over which their jurisdiction reached. For many years their principal duties were confined to measures for carrying on local improvements. It was considered "requisite, for the maintenance of good order and the rigid execution of the laws, that proper officers should be appointed to superintend the observance thereof."[1] Accordingly, the people were authorized by statute to meet in any parish, township or reputed township or place on the warrant of the High-Constable, who was to preside on such occasions. These assemblies were composed of the inhabitants who were householders and ratepayers in the locality interested, and were held in the early times, for convenience sake, in the parish church or chapel. They had to elect a parish or town Clerk, who was to make out annual lists of the inhabitants within a district, keep the records, and perform other business connected with such an office. The other officers appointed were as follows: Assessors, to assess all such rates and taxes "as shall be imposed by any Act or Acts of the Legislature;" a Collector, "to receive such taxes and rates in the manner authorised by the Legislature;" Overseers of Roads and Highways, "to oversee and perform such things as shall be directed by any act passed touching or concerning the highways and roads in the province," and to act as Fence-Viewers "conformable to any resolutions that may be agreed upon by the inhabitants at such meetings"; a Pound-Keeper, to impound all stray cattle. The act also provided for two Town-Wardens. As soon as there should be any church built for the performance of Divine service according to the use of the Church of England, then the parson or minister was to nominate one Warden and the inhabitants the other. These Wardens were a corporation to represent the whole inhabitants of the township or parish, with the right to let or sell property, to sue and be sued. The High-Constable, who called and presided over the township meetings, was appointed by the Justices in

[1] Upp. Can. Stat. 33 Geo. III, c. 2.

Quarter-Sessions. The presiding officer had to communicate a list of persons nominated at these meetings to a Magistrate, who was to administer to them the oath of office. In case the persons appointed at the meeting refused to act, they were subject to a penalty, and the Magistrates in Sessions called for that purpose proceeded to fill the vacancies. In case there were not thirty inhabitants in a township, then they were considered to form part of the adjacent township which should contain the smallest number of inhabitants.[1]

The following extract from the early records of the township of Sophiasburg, or the 6th township lying on Picton and Quinté Bays, will be read with interest, because it shows that there was an attempt made to establish a parish system on the basis of that so long existent in the parent State. No similar record can be found in the annals of the old townships of Upper Canada, although the references in the Constitutional Act of 1791, and in several provincial statutes,[2] go to show that the erection of parishes was in the minds of those who were engaged in developing local institutions in the country:—

"Passed at Sophiasburg, at a regular town meeting, 3rd March, 1800. And be it observed—That all well-regulated townships be divided into parishes. Be it enacted by the

---

[1] One of the first reported town meetings (Canniff, p. 454) held in accordance with the act, was that of Adolphustown, which came off on the 6th of March, 1793. The following words are an exact transcript of the record:— "The following persons were chosen to officiate in their respective offices, the ensuing year, and also the regulations of the same: Reuben Bedell, township clerk; Paul Huff and Philip Dorland, overseers of the poor; Joseph Allison and Garit Benson, constables; Willet Casey, Paul Huff and John Huyck, Pound-Keepers; Abraham Maybee and Peter Rutland, Fence-Viewers. The height of fence to be 4 feet 8 inches; water fence voted to be no fence. Hoggs running at large to have yokes on 18 by 24 inches. No piggs to run until three months old. No stallion to run. Any person putting fire to any bush or stable, that does not his endeavour to hinder it from doing damage, shall forfeit the sum of forty shillings."

(Signed) Philip Dorland, T. Clerk.

[2] See *supra*, p. 58.

majority of votes, that this town shall be divided into parishes, and described as follows: St. John's, St. Matthew's, St. Giles, Mount Pleasant."[1]

It does not appear, however, that parishes were established to any extent on the English system throughout Upper Canada, although they were general for ecclesiastical purposes. The Church of England was the dominant religious body for many years, and there was an effort made to establish it by giving it large reserves of public lands. We shall see, however, later on, that parishes were established in the maritime provinces for civil purposes as in some of the old English colonies in America.

In accordance with the British system of local government in counties, the Magistrates in Sessions performed an important part in the administration of local affairs. These Courts of Quarter Sessions have long existed in English counties, and their functions have been regulated by a series of statutes commencing in the Tudor times and coming down to the present day. The English counties were subdivided into petty sessional divisions. At the head of this civil organization in a county is the Lord-Lieutenant and the *Custos Rotulorum.* These two offices are usually held by one person, who holds office under a special commission from the Crown, and is generally a peer of the realm or large landowner.[2] "His office," says Hallam, "may be considered as a revival of the ancient local earldom, and it certainly took away from the sheriff a great part of the dignity and importance which he had acquired since the discontinuance of that office. Yet the Lord-Lieutenant has so peculiarly military an authority that it does not in any degree control the civil power of the sheriff as the executive minister of the law."[3]

---

[1] Canniff, p. 472.

[2] The English Citizen Series. Local Government in England, M. D. Chalmers, p. 93.

[3] Const. Hist. (Eng. ed. 1881) ii. 134.

It appears from the old records that there was a similar officer appointed in the early times of Canada. Speaking of Lower Canada, Lord Durham says: "The Justices of the Peace scattered over the whole of Lower Canada are named by the Governor on no very accurate information, there being no Lieutenants or similar officers of counties in this as in the upper province."[1] The Duke de la Rochefoucault, writing in 1795, says: "Simcoe is by no means ambitious of investing all power and authority in his own hands, but consents that the *Lieutenants*, whom he nominates for each county, should appoint the Justices of the Peace and the officers of the militia."[2] From these and other references to the duties of the officer, he appears to have discharged functions similar to those of the Lord-Lieutenant in England, since he appointed Justices and commanded the militia. The title, however, appears to have fallen into disuse in the course of a few years,[3] though there was a Custos Rotulorum or Chairman of Sessions in all the provinces. The Lieutenancy in Upper Canada never assumed as much importance as did the same office in Virginia.[4]

---

[1] Report, p. 41.

[2] Vol. i. p. 416.

[3] The *Upper Canada Almanac* for 1804, published at York, gives the following list of "Lieutenants of Counties:" "John Macdonell, Esq., Glengarry; William Fortune, Esq., Prescott; Archibald Macdonell, Esq., Stormont; Hon. Richard Duncan, Esq., Dundas; Peter Drummond, Esq., Grenville; James Breckenridge, Esq., Leeds; Hon. Richard Cartwright, Esq., Frontenac; Hazelton Spencer, Esq., Lenox; William Johnson, Esq., Addington; John Ferguson, Esq., Hastings; Archibald Macdonell, Esq., of Marysburg, Prince Edward; Alexander Chisholm, Esq., Northumberland; Robert Baldwin, Esq., Durham; Hon. David William Smith, Esq., York; Hon. Robert Hamilton, Esq., Lincoln; Samuel Ryerse, Esq., Norfolk; William Claus, Esq., Oxford; (Middlesex vacant); Hon. Alexander Grant, Esq., Essex; Hon. James Baby, Kent." These Lieutenants do not appear to have been appointed in subsequent years. The foregoing list recalls the names of men prominent in the early days of Canada. Some of their descendants still play a conspicuous part in public affairs.

[4] "One is struck by the prominence of the Lieutenant, anciently the Commander, who, besides being the chief of the militia in his county, was a

As I have already shown, the Justices in sessions appointed as in England a High Constable, and discharged certain functions now performed by municipal bodies in Canada. All moneys collected by Assessors of Taxes were to be paid into the hands of Treasurers who were appointed by the Justices in general quarter sessions. The Justices so assembled directed how the moneys were to be disbursed in accordance with the law. The Legislature, from time to time, regulated the time and place for holding these Courts. The Quarter-Sessions were held in 1793, at Adolphustown, Kingstown, Michillimackinac, Newark, New Johnstown, and Cornwall, then the principal towns of the province. The jurisdiction of the Justices was very extensive in those times. They had the carrying out in a great measure of the Acts of the Legislature providing for the defraying of the expenses of building court-houses and jails, of keeping the same in repair, of the payment of Jailers, of the support and maintenance of prisons, of the building and repairing of houses of correction, of the construction and repairs of bridges, of the fees of Coroners and other officers, and of all other matters that were essentially of a local character. Whenever it was necessary to establish a market, the Legislature had to pass a special Act giving the requisite power to the Court of Sessions. For instance, we find an Act authorizing the Justices in this Court "to fix, open and establish some convenient place in the town of Kingston as a market, where butcher's meat, butter, eggs, poultry, fish and vegetables, shall be exposed to sale, and to appoint such days and hours as shall be suitable for that purpose, and to make such other orders and regulations relative thereto as they shall deem expedient."[1] The Justices of the

---

member of the Council, and as such a judge of the highest tribunal in the county. With Commissioners of the Governor he held monthly courts for the settlement of suits, not exceeding in value one hundred pounds of tobacco, and from this court, appeal was allowed to the Governor and Council." Local Institutions of Virginia. By Edw. Ingle, Johns Hopkins University Studies in Historical and Political Science, vol. iii. 185.

[1] Upp. Can. Stat. 41 Geo. III, c. 3.

Peace had also other important functions to discharge out of the sessions. For instance, it was on their certificate that the Secretary of State granted licenses to public houses. These licenses were only granted after full inquiry and discussion at public meetings duly called for that purpose by the High Constable or other public officer.[1] The Justices in quarter sessions also appointed Surveyors of Highways, to lay out and regulate statute labor on the public roads. All persons were liable to work on the roads, in proportion to the assessment on their real and personal property.[2]

For the first fifteen or twenty years of the history of the administration of civil affairs in Upper Canada, the burdens of the people were exceedingly small. A Canadian historian says on this point: "No civilized country in the world was less burdened with taxes than Canada West at this period. A small direct tax on property, levied by the District Courts of Sessions, and not amounting to £3,500 for the whole country, sufficed for all local expenses. There was no poor rate, no capitation tax, no tithes, no ecclesiastical rates of any kind. Instead of a road tax, a few days of statute labor annually sufficed."[3]

Under such circumstances we can easily understand why the condition of Kingston, for many years the most important town of Upper Canada, should have been so pitiable according to a writer of those early times: "The streets [in 1815] require very great repairs, as in the rainy seasons it is scarcely possible to move about without being in mud to the ankles. Lamps are required. . . . But first the Legislature must form a code of laws, forming a complete police. To meet expense, Government might lay a rate upon every inhabitant householder in proportion to value of property in house."[4]

---

[1] Upp. Can. Stat. 34 Geo. III, c. 12.

[2] *Ibid.*, 48 Geo. III, c. 12.

[3] McMullen's History, p. 247.

[4] Canniff, p. 432.

Subsequently, when Kingston became the seat of government, the municipal authorities were encouraged to make improvements in streets, drainage, sidewalks, and otherwise. When the town of York was incorporated as a city, in 1834, under the name of Toronto, it had not a single sidewalk within its limits, and the first Mayor, Mr. W. Lyon Mackenzie, had to initiate a system of local improvements under great difficulties.[1]

As the country filled up, and the necessity arose for roads and bridges and other local improvements, the taxes increased; although they never became heavy under the unsatisfactory system that prevailed, until after the reunion of the Canadas in 1841. The time of the Legislature was constantly occupied in passing Acts for the construction of public works necessary for the comfort, safety, and convenience of particular localities. A large amount of "parish" business was transacted in those days by the Legislature which might as well have been done by local Councils. As compared with Lower Canada, however, the people had eventually a workable system of local government, which enabled them to make many improvements for themselves. The construction of canals and other important works of provincial importance, on an expensive scale, at last left so little funds in the treasury that the Parliament of this province alone, among the North American colonies "was, fortunately for itself, compelled to establish a system of local assessment, and to leave local works in a great measure to the energy and means of the localities themselves."[2] Still the system, as the country became more populous and enterprising, proved ultimately quite inadequate to meet the requirements of the people and to develop their latent energies. The Legislature was constantly called upon to give power to local authorities to carry out measures of local necessity. Whatever taxation was necessary for local purposes had to be im-

---

[1] Lindsey's Life of Mackenzie, i. 312.

[2] Lord Durham's Report, p. 48.

posed through the inconvenient agency of Courts of Quarter-Sessions, over which the people exercised little or no control. If the people of a city or town wished to be incorporated, they were forced to apply to the Legislature for a special Act. The powers granted to these corporations were by no means uniform, and great confusion resulted from the many statutes that existed with respect to these bodies. "No lawyer," says a writer on the subject,[1] could give an opinion upon the rights of an individual in a single corporation without following the original act through the thousand sinuosities of parliamentary amendment, and no capitalist at a distance could credit a city or town without a particular and definite acquaintance with its individual history." It was not, however, until after the reunion of the Canadian provinces, that steps were taken to establish in Upper Canada a larger system of popular local government in accordance with the wise suggestions made by Lord Durham and other sagacious British statesmen. But before we can refer to this part of the subject, I must first review the early local history of the maritime provinces of Nova Scotia, New Brunswick, and Prince Edward Island.

V.—The Maritime Provinces.

When Nova Scotia became a possession of England by the treaty of Utrecht in 1713, the only place of any importance was Port Royal, originally founded by a French gentleman-adventurer, Baron de Poutrincourt. The English renamed the place "Annapolis Royal," in honor of Queen Anne, and for some years it was the seat of government. The province in those days had a considerable French Acadian population, chiefly settled in the Annapolis valley, and in the fertile country watered by the streams that flow into the Bay of Fundy. For some years there was a military government in Nova Scotia. In 1719, the governor received instructions to choose a council

[1] J. Sheridan Hogan, Prize Essay on Canada, 1855, p. 104.

for the management of civil affairs from the principal English inhabitants, until an assembly should be formed to regulate matters in accordance with the instructions given to the American colonies generally. This first council was composed exclusively of officers of the garrison and of officials of the public departments. The French inhabitants in their respective parishes were permitted, in the absence of duly appointed magistrates, to choose deputies from among themselves for the purpose of executing the orders of the government and acting as arbitrators in case of controversies in the French settlements. An appeal was allowed to the governor at Annapolis.[1]

In 1749, the city of Halifax was founded by Governor Cornwallis on the shores of Chebucto Bay, on the Atlantic coast. The government of the province was vested in a Governor and Council, and one of their first acts was to establish a Court of General Sessions, similar in its nature and conformable in its practice to the Courts of the same name in the parent State.[2] In 1751 they passed an ordinance that the town and suburbs of Halifax be divided into eight wards, and the inhabitants empowered to choose annually the following officials "for managing such prudential affairs of the town as shall be committed to their care by the Governor and Council:—eight town-overseers, one town-clerk, sixteen constables, eight scavengers."[3]

It was only after the establishment of the first Legislature that Nova Scotia was divided into local divisions for legislative, judicial, and civil purposes. The first House of Assembly, elected in 1758, was composed of twenty-two representatives, of whom sixteen were chosen by the province at large, four by the township of Halifax, and two by the township of Lunenburg. It was at the same time provided that whenever fifty

[1] Haliburton's History of Nova Scotia, i. 93, 96.

[2] *Ibid.*, p. 163.

[3] Murdoch's History, ii. 199.

qualified householders were settled at Pisiquid (now Windsor), Minas, Cobequid, or at any other township which might be thereafter erected, it should be entitled to send two representatives to the Assembly.[1] In 1759, the Governor and Council divided the province into five counties: Annapolis, Kings, Cumberland, Lunenburg and Halifax.[2] A few years later the whole island of Cape Breton was formed into a county.[3]

The Legislature appears to have practically controlled the administration of local affairs throughout the province, except so far as it gave, from time to time, certain powers to the Courts of Quarter-Sessions to regulate taxation and carry out certain public works and improvements. In the first session of the Legislature, a joint committee of the Council and Assembly choose the town officers for Halifax, viz., four overseers of the poor, two clerks of the market, four surveyors of the highways, two fence viewers, and two hog-reeves.[4] We have abundant evidence that at this time the authorities viewed with disfavor any attempt to establish a system of town government similar to that so long in operation in New England. On the 14th of April, 1770, the Governor and Council passed a resolution that "the proceedings of the people in calling town-meetings for discussing questions relative to law and government and such other purposes, are contrary to law, and if persisted in, it is ordered that the parties be prosecuted by the attorney-general."[5] The government of Nova Scotia had before it, at this time, the example of the town-meetings of Boston, presided over by the famous Samuel Adams, and

---

[1] Haliburton, i. 208. Murdoch, ii. 334, 351.

[2] Murdoch, ii. 373, 374. In the election for the Assembly that came off in August of the same year, the counties in question returned two members each; the towns of Lunenburg, Annapolis, Horton, and Cumberland, two each, and the township of Halifax, four, or twenty-two representatives in all.

[3] *Ibid.*, p. 454.

[4] *Ibid.*, p. 361.

[5] Haliburton, i. 248.

doubtless considered them as the very hotbeds of revolution.[1] What the Tories thought of these popular bodies can be understood from the following extract, which gives the opinion of a rabid writer of those revolutionary times. "This is the foulest, subtlest, and most enormous serpent ever issued from the egg of sedition. I saw the small seed when it was implanted; it was a grain of mustard. I have watched the plant until it has become a great tree."[2]

In the course of time the province was divided for legislative, judicial and civil purposes, as follows:—

1. Divisions or circuits, generally consisting of one or more counties, for purposes connected with the Courts.
2. Districts, generally of one or more counties, established, as a rule, for the convenience of the people, who had the privilege conferred upon them of having a Court of Sessions of the Peace for the regulation of their internal affairs.
3. Counties, generally established for legislative purposes.
4. Townships, which were simply subdivisions of the county intended for purposes of local administration or of representation.

In each county there was a Sheriff and Justice of the Peace, whose jurisdiction extended throughout the same. Each district was generally provided with a Court-house which belonged to the county. The townships did not contain any definite quantity of land, as was generally the case in Upper Canada. The inhabitants appear, according to Judge Haliburton, "to have had no other power than that of holding an

---

[1] Bancroft very truly considers Samuel Adams more than any other man, "the type and representative of the New England town-meeting." History of the Constitution, ii. 260. For an interesting account of his career, see Samuel Adams, the Man of the Town Meeting, by J. K. Hosmer. Here the reader will be able to obtain a very accurate idea of the important influence that Adams and the town-meetings of Boston exercised over the destinies of America. No wonder was it that the governing class in Halifax frowned upon all manifestations of popular feeling in the province.

[2] Daniel Leonard, cited by Hosmer, p. 45.

annual meeting for the purpose of voting money for the support of the poor."[1] Up to very recent times, the Justices in Sessions were practically the local governing bodies in the various divisions of the province. Even Halifax was not allowed a special act of incorporation as a city until 1841, although its people made frequent applications to the Legislature for power to manage their own affairs.[2] The time of the Legislature was taken up with making provision for local wants. All the roads and bridges were built and maintained, and the public schools supported by the Legislature. The system that so long prevailed, by which members of the Legislature controlled the expenditures for local works, was well calculated to demoralize public men and encourage speculation and jobbery. Large sums were frittered away by the appointment of Road Commissioners with reference only to political considerations.[3] It was one well adapted to stimulate the energies of village politicians, and the spirit of party in the counties.

As respects local affairs, the people had little or no voice. The Grand Jury, in the Court of Sessions of the Peace,

---

[1] Haliburton's Hist. ii. 8, 9.

[2] Murdoch, ii. 449. In 1850 Mr. Howe attempted to pass a bill dividing the county of Halifax into townships, and conferring certain municipal privileges upon the inhabitants. The people were to have the power to raise funds by assessment for the support of education and for other public purposes, and to elect their own township officers, including Magistrates. Lord Grey, however, took exception to the measure, and the Queen's assent was withheld. Speeches and Public Letters of Hon. Joseph Howe, i. 642.

[3] "According to a report presented to me by Major Head, an Assistant Commissioner of Enquiry whom I sent to that colony [Nova Scotia], a sum of £10,000 was, during the last session, appropriated to local improvements; this sum was divided into 830 portions, and as many Commissioners were appointed to expend it, giving, on an average, a Commissioner for rather more than every £12, with a salary of 5s. a day, and a further remuneration of two and a half per cent. on the money expended, to be deducted out of each share." Lord Durham's Report, p. 29. This demoralizing and wasteful system lasted until very recently in Nova Scotia.

annually nominated such number of town officers as the Justices should direct, and out of them the latter made the appointments. The Grand Jury had also the power to raise money for certain public purposes within a particular division. Of their own knowledge, or on the representation of three freeholders, they could make presentments for money for building or repairing jails, court-houses, pounds, or for other necessary local purposes. In the event of their neglecting to act, in certain cases the Justices in Sessions could amerce the county. The officers appointed at the Sessions were a County Treasurer and Assessors. The Clerk of the Peace, as in England, was appointed by the Custos, as Chairman of the Sessions; the office of Sheriff was a government appointment. Practically, in Nova Scotia, as in the other provinces, the English county system prevailed.

If we now turn to the province of New Brunswick, we find that a similar system existed until very recently. This province originally formed part of the extensive and ill-defined territory known in French times as "Acadie." For some years it was governed by the Governor and Council of Nova Scotia, until the settlement of a large number of Loyalists on the banks of the St. John River brought about a change in its political constitution. Then the Imperial authorities thought it expedient to create a separate province, with a government consisting, in the first instance, of a Governor and Council of twelve members, exercising both executive and legislative powers, and, eventually, of an assembly of twenty-six members.

On the 17th of May, 1785, a charter was granted by Governor Carleton for the incorporation of Parr Town, on the east side of the St. John River, and of Carleton, on the west side, as a city under the name of St. John.[1] The inhabitants

---

[1] "The Governor of Nova Scotia—which then included New Brunswick—at the time of the arrival of the Loyalists, was John Parr, Esq., and St. John was at first named *Parr Town*, after that gentleman." Jack's Prize Essay on the History of St. John, p. 65.

were given a Mayor, Recorder, six Alderman and six assistants, and the city was divided into six wards.[1] St. John, consequently, was the first city incorporated in British North America, and it remained so for many years, as Halifax and other towns were refused the same privileges for a long while.

In 1786 the Governor, Council and Assembly passed an act providing that the Justices of the General Sessions of the Peace for the several counties of the province should annually appoint, out of every town or parish in the same, Overseers, Clerk, Constables, Clerks of Markets, Assessors, Surveyors, Weighers of Hay, Fence Viewers. It will be seen from this and other acts that the divisions for local purposes consisted of counties, townships and parishes. In 1786, an act was passed for the better ascertaining and confirming of the boundaries of the several counties[2] within the province, and for subdividing them into towns or parishes "for the more convenient and orderly distribution of the respective inhabitants, to enable them, in their respective districts, to fulfil the several duties incumbent on them, and for the better administration of justice therein."

Town and *parish* appear to have been always synonymous terms in this province. In the interpretation clause of a recent act, "parish" is defined as "*parish*, incorporated town or city."[3] This designation of one of the civil divisions of New Brunswick is, no doubt, so much evidence of the desire of the early settlers, many of whom were from Virginia and Maryland,[4] to introduce the institutions of their old homes.

---

[1] Murdoch, iii. 42.

[2] "The names of the original eight counties into which New Brunswick was divided, are: Saint John, Westmoreland, York, Charlotte, Northumberland, King's, Queen's, and Sunbury. These counties were confirmed by law February 10th, 1786." Jack's Prize Essay, p. 74.

[3] N. B. Cons. Stat., c. 100, s. i.

[4] Among the members of the first Council of New Brunswick, 1784, were Chief Justice Ludlow, formerly a Judge of the Supreme Court of New York; Judge Israel Allen, of Pennsylvania; Gabriel G. Ludlow, of Maryland; Judge John Saunders, of Virginia. Not a few Virginia Loyalists settled in New Brunswick. Murdoch, iii. 42.

In all of the British colonies, indeed, the town system had long been in use. In the first instance, the colonists introduced the local institutions of the parent State, with such modifications as were suitable to the conditions of their existence. But the "parish" of the colonies, as a rule, bore little resemblance to the historic "parish" of England. The latter was simply the old township of the Saxons in an ecclesiastical form: "The district assigned to a church or priest; to whom its ecclesiastical dues and generally also its tithes are paid. The boundaries of the parish and the township or townships with which it coincides, are generally the same; in small parishes the idea and even name of township is frequently, at the present day, sunk in that of the parish; and all the business that is not manorial is despatched in vestry meetings, which are however primarily meetings of the township for church purposes."[1]

Throughout New England the township was the political unit. It is true that the religious convictions of the people dominated in all their arrangements for the administration of civil affairs. An eminent authority has said of the people of Massachusetts: "They founded a civil state upon a basis which should support the worship of God according to their conscientious convictions of duty; and an ecclesiastical state combined with it, which should sustain and be in harmony with the civil government, excluding what was antagonistic to the welfare of either."[2] In England the parish was invested with civil functions, and the old Saxon township became gradually absorbed in the former. But in New England the parish and township had really distinct meanings. Whenever the word "parish" was there used, it was to denote the township from an ecclesiastical point of view, as well as a portion of the township not possessing town rights. Consequently the "parish of Massachusetts" was essentially a term used for religious

[1] Stubbs, Const. Hist. i. 85.

[2] Parker's Lowell Institute Lectures, p. 403.

purposes, and had no reference to civil matters which were all discharged in the township or political unit of the community.[1] In Virginia, however, the parish attained considerable prominence in the administration of local affairs. The early settlers of the old Dominion were men wedded to the ancient institutions of the parent State, and they set up the system long established in England, with such changes as were adapted to the circumstances of the country. Parishes were originally coterminous with the old plantations or with the counties, and covered immense areas. In the course of time, when the country became more settled, counties were laid out and divided into parishes. Some of these parishes sent representatives to the House of Burgesses in early times of the colony, and they were always important local units in the civil organization of the country. It does not, however, appear that they ever possessed powers entirely equal to those enjoyed in the parent State.[2] No doubt the Loyalists who settled in New Brunswick and other sections of British North America were so accustomed to this division that they naturally introduced it when they came to organize the new province. We have already seen, in our sketch of local government in Upper Canada, that there was an effort made to establish parishes in that section. It is only in New Brunswick, however, that the name has become permanently inscribed on the civil organization of the country. I do not of course refer in this connection to French Canada, where the division was constituted purely for ecclesiastical purposes, and had no relation to the English parish which is the descendant of the township of early English times—itself developed from the mark communities of the Teutonic tribes.[3]

---

[1] The English Parish in America; Local Institutions in Virginia, by E. Ingle, Johns Hopkins University Studies, vol. iii. 154.

[2] Johns Hopkins University Studies, vol. iii. 154, 155.

[3] "Primarily the parish is merely the old township in its ecclesiastical aspect. We can, therefore, trace the descent of the modern civil parish through the ecclesiastical parish, up to the old Saxon township. It may

The Island of Prince Edward, originally known as St. John's, formed part of the province of Nova Scotia until 1769, when it was created a separate province, with a Lieutenant-Governor, a combined Executive and Legislative Council, and in 1773 a Legislative Assembly of eighteen members.[1] The history of this island is interesting from the fact that it gives an instance of a land system which kept the province in a state of agitation for many years, until it was finally settled soon after the union with the Dominion. The island was surveyed by Captain Holland in 1765, and in 1767 divided into sixty-seven townships, containing in the aggregate 1,360,600 acres.[2] This extensive tract was conveyed by ballot, with some reservations, to officers and other individuals who had claims or supposed claims on the Crown, and a landed monopoly was in this way established in the island. The grantees were to settle in the province or establish a certain number of settlers within ten years, but these proper conditions were practically laid aside and an absentee ownership allowed to grow up, to the great injury of the tenants who farmed the lands. In those days the Crown availed itself lavishly of its prerogatives with very little regard to future settlement on the public lands of the country over which it exercised dominion. Previous to the arrangement

---

be safely said that the English parish is the legitimate descendant of the Teutonic mark, and that the English parish, the New England township, the French or Belgian commune, and the village community of Northern India, are but variations of one common type which reproduces itself wherever the Aryan race is found. Whether the Teutonic mark system was ever introduced into England by our Saxon forefathers is an open question, but the Saxon township owed many of its distinguishing characteristics to the mark system. The township was so called from the *tun* or hedge which surrounded the group of homesteads." Chalmers' Local Government in England, p. 36.

[1] Bourinot, p. 69. See also copy of commission of the first Lieutenant-Governor, Captain W. Paterson. Canada Sessional Papers, 1883, No. 70, p. 2.

[2] Campbell's History, pp. 3, 19. Colonial Office List, 1885, p. 38.

just mentioned, a British nobleman had applied to the King for a grant of the whole island. His proposition was to divide it into hundreds[1] as in England, or baronies as in Ireland. These hundreds or baronies were to be divided into manors over which would preside a Court Baron, in accordance with the old English system. Townships were to be carved out of hundreds; Courts Leet and Courts Baron were also to be established under the direction of the lord paramount. A local historian has clearly epitomized the whole proposition as follows: "There was to be a lord paramount of the whole island, forty capital lords of forty hundreds, four hundred lords of manors, and eight hundred freeholders. For assurance of the said tenures, eight hundred thousand acres were to be set apart for establishments for trade and commerce in the most suitable parts of the island, including one county town, forty market towns, and four hundred villages." Each hundred or barony was to consist of somewhat less than eight square miles, and the lord of each was bound to erect and maintain forever a castle or blockhouse as the capital seat of his property, and as a place of retreat and rendezvous for the settlers; and thus, on any alarm of sudden danger, every inhabitant might have a place of security within four miles of his habitation. A cannon

---

[1] It does not appear that "hundreds" were ever established in Canada. The union of a number of townships for the purpose of judicial administration, peace and defence, formed what is known as the *hundred* or *wapentake*, in Anglo-Saxon times. "It is very probable," writes Stubbs (i. 96, 97) "that the colonists of Britain arranged themselves in hundreds of warriors; it is not probable that the country was carved into equal districts. The only conclusion that seems reasonable is that, under the name of geographical hundreds, we have the variously sized *pagi* or districts in which the hundred warriors settled." The first civil divisions of the infant settlement of Maryland were called "hundreds," and the election district of "Bay Hundred" on the eastern shore of the State, is a memorial of those old times. Local Institutions of Maryland, by L. W. Wilhelm, p. 39. A similar division was also known in the early history of Virginia. Ingle, pp. 40–47.

fired at one of the castles would be heard at the next, and thus the firing would proceed in regular order from castle to castle, and be "the means," adds the noble memoralist, "of putting every inhabitant of the whole island under arms and in motion in the space of one quarter of an hour."[1]

But this proposition was not entertained by the King, who had had some experience of a similar plan which failed in Carolina.[2] The division, however, of the whole island, among a few proprietors, appears to have had consequences probably fully as disastrous as would have been the concession to a single nobleman, who might have taken a deep interest in its settlement, as was notably done by Lord Baltimore in Maryland.

The island was originally laid out in counties,[3] parishes, and townships. The county lines appear to have been run from north to south across the island at two of its widest parts. Where the boundaries of townships or parishes touch the county lines, they are coterminous therewith. The same is true of the township and parish lines. The average area of the townships is 20,000 acres, though number 66, the last regular township surveyed, contains only 6,000, and number 67, an irregular block in the centre of the island, is somewhat larger than the average.

Each parish includes from three to six townships. In addition to the territorial divisions before mentioned, there was laid out in each county, at the time of the original survey,

---

[1] Campbell's History, ch. i. p. 11.

[2] Shaftesbury and Locke attempted to frame a constitution for Carolina, which would "connect political power with hereditary wealth." Bancroft's History of the United States, ii. 146.

[3] "In 1768 the Island was divided into three counties:—(1.) King's, containing 20 townships, 412,100 acres; county town, Georgetown, 4,000 acres (Les Trois Rivières). (2.) Queen's, 23 townships, 486,600 acres; county town, Charlottetown, 7,300 acres (Port la Joie). (3.) Prince County, 23 townships, 467,000 acres; county town, Princetown, 4,000 acres (Malpeque)." Murdoch's History, ii. 474. The names in parentheses are those of the old French settlements.

a site for a *chef lieu*, or county town. For Queen's County, a town plot was laid out on the site of the present city of Charlottetown, at the head of Hillsboro' Bay, where the North-West and Hillsboro' Rivers unite. The town of King's County was laid out at Georgetown, on the south-east coast, on Cardigan Bay, and, for Prince County, a town site was surveyed on the east side of Richmond or Malpeque Bay, near its mouth. To each of these town sites there were attached distinct areas of land called "commons"[1] and "royalties,"[2] which covered about 6,000 acres each, and were not included in any of the townships. Instead of being reserved for their original purpose, the common and royalty attached to each town site were subsequently sold by the Crown as farm lands, and are now occupied and cultivated as such, though the city of Charlottetown extends beyond the old town site, and covers a portion of the common. The county town of Prince County was not established at Princetown, but at a point on the shores of Bedeque Bay, on the south coast, now called "Summerside."

As we have just seen, there was an attempt made in Prince Edward Island to establish parishes as in other parts of the old colonies, but, in the course of time, these local divisions became practically useless, and are seldom mentioned now, except in legal proceedings connected with old land titles. It is only in Prince Edward Island, I may add, that we come across the term "royalties" as reservations of the crown, in

---

[1] These common lands were a memorial of Anglo-Saxon times. "The pleasant green commons or squares which occur in the midst of towns and cities in England and the United States most probably originated from the coalescence of adjacent mark-communities, whereby the border-land used in common by all was brought into the centre of the new aggregate. . . . In old towns of New England. . . . the little park. . . . was once the common pasture of the town."—Fiske's American Political Ideas, pp. 39, 40.

[2] "In its primary and natural sense 'royalties' is merely the English translation or equivalent of *regalitates, jura regalia, jura regia.*" See an interesting definition of the term given by the Judicial Committee of the Privy Council, Legal News (Montreal), vi. 244; and Bourinot, p. 690.

the vicinity of the old settlements. In the other provinces, however, provision was made for the establishment of commons,[1] though, in the course of time, they, too, in the majority of cases, were leased for private purposes and ceased to become available for the general use of the community. The Legislature of Nova Scotia, for instance, passed an act in 1816 to lease twenty-five acres of the Halifax common, in half acre lots, for 999 years.[2]

In this island, the several divisions to which we have referred appear to have been established chiefly for representative and judicial purposes. No system of local government ever existed in the counties and parishes, as in other parts of America. The Legislature has been always a municipal council for the whole island.

VI.—The Establishment of Municipal Institutions in the Provinces of the Dominion.

We have now brought this review of local government up to the time when a new era in the history of political institutions commenced in all the provinces of British North America. The troubles which culminated in the Rebellion of 1837-8 led to the reunion of the Canadas and the concession of a more liberal system of government to the people. The British authorities recognized the necessity of leaving the people free to control their own internal affairs, and of giving up that system of paternal government which had worked so unsatisfactorily. Between 1840 and 1854 all the provinces were granted responsible government in the real sense of the term, and entered almost immediately on a career of political and national progress which was in remarkable contrast with the condition of things previous to 1840. The legislation of the province was distinguished by greater vigor as soon as the

[1] Nova Scotia Archives, Aikens, p. 700.

[2] Murdoch, iii. 415.

people obtained full control of their own taxation and revenue. The result was the improvement of the communications of the country and the passage of measures in the direction of increasing the responsibilities of the people in the management of their local affairs.

In the speech with which Lord Sydenham, then Governor-General, opened the Legislature of 1841, he called attention to the fact that it was "highly desirable that the principles of local self-government, which already prevail to some extent throughout that part of the province which was formerly Upper Canada, should receive a more extended application and that the people should exercise a greater control over their own local affairs."[1] It had been proposed to make such a system a part of the Constitution of 1840;[2] but the clauses on the subject were struck out of the bill during its passage in the House of Commons on the ground that such a purely local matter should be left to the Legislature of the province.[3] The Legislature went energetically to work to provide for the

---

[1] Assembly Journals, 1841, p. 8.

[2] "The establishment of a good system of municipal institutions throughout these provinces is a matter of vital importance. A general legislature, which manages the private business of every parish, in addition to the common business of the county, wields a power which no single body, however popular in its constitution, ought to have—a power which must be destructive of any constitutional balance. The true principle of limiting popular power is that apportionment of it in many different depositories, which has been adopted in all the most free and stable States of the Union. Instead of confiding the whole collection and distribution of all the revenues raised in any county for all general and local purposes to a single representative body, the power of local assessment, and the application of the funds arising from it, should be intrusted to local management. It is in vain to expect that this sacrifice of power will be voluntarily made by any representative body. The establishment of municipal institutions for the whole country should be made a part of every colonial constitution, and the prerogative of the Crown should be constantly interposed to check any encroachment on the functions of the local bodies, until the people should become alive, as most assuredly they almost immediately would be, to the necessity of protecting their local privileges." Lord Durham's Report, p. 92.

[3] Christie, v. 356.

internal government of the upper province. Some difficulties arose in dealing with this question on account of the position taken by Lower Canada. During the suspension of the Constitution in French Canada, an ordinance had been passed by the Special Council "to provide for the better internal government of this province by the establishment of local or municipal institutions therein." The province was divided into twenty-two districts, comprising certain seigniories, townships, and parishes. The Governor and Council fixed and determined the number of Councillors who were elected for every district. The warden was appointed by the Governor-General, and his duties were regulated by instructions from the same high functionary. The meetings of householders, at which the parish or township officers as well as the district Councillors were elected and other business was transacted, were convened on the authorization of the warden by one of the Justices of the Peace for the district. The Governor had the power to dissolve a district Council under extraordinary circumstances. Instructions were issued by the Governor and Council to the chairmen of parish or township meetings, assessors, collectors, surveyors of highways and bridges, overseers of the poor, and other local officers.[1]

Consequently, the system in operation in Lower Canada was entirely controlled by the government. It was the desire of the Upper Canadians, who had been gradually educated for more popular local institutions, to elect the warden and other officers. The measure which was presented in 1841, by Mr. Harrison, provincial secretary of the upper province, provided that the inhabitants of each district should be a body corporate within the limits prescribed by the Act, and provision was made for the formation of municipal councils, to consist of a warden and a fixed number of councillors in each district. Power was given to these councils to assess and collect from the inhabitants such moneys as might be necessary

[1] Canada Sessional Papers, 1841, App. X.

for local purposes, and generally to adopt measures for the good government of the respective districts represented in these local bodies. The Upper Canadians naturally wished to elect their own Warden, but it was argued that it was inexpedient to concede to one province privileges not given to the other. The French members in the legislature were not only opposed to the measure passed by the special council, but believed that, if they sanctioned the passage of a liberal measure in Upper Canada, it would be followed by similar legislation for Lower Canada. The most influential men in that province were opposed at that time to any system that might impose local direct taxation on the people.[1]

Imperfect as was the Act of 1841, it was the commencement of a new era in municipal government in Canada. In the course of a few years the Act was amended, and the people at last obtained full control of the election of their own municipal officers. Statutes passed from time to time swept away those numerous corporate bodies which had been established by the legislature of the old province, and provided by one general law "for the erection of municipal corporations and the establishment of police regulations in and for the several counties, cities, towns, townships and villages in Upper Canada."[2] Lower Canada was also brought into the general system, according as the people began to comprehend the advantages of controlling their local affairs. The ordinance of the special council was repealed in 1845 by an Act, which provided that every township or parish should constitute a municipal corporation, represented by a council elected by the people, and presided over by a President or Mayor, also elective.[3] This parish organization seemed peculiarly well adapted to the habits of the people of French Canada, where the parish is connected with their dearest and most interesting associations; but for

---

[1] Dent's Canada since the Union of 1841, i. 146.
[2] Con. Stat. 12 Vict. c. 80, and 12 Vict. c. 81.
[3] Turcotte, Canada sous l'Union, ii. 24.

some reason or other it was soon changed to a county government, which lasted for a number of years.[1] Without, however, dwelling on the numerous acts which occupied considerable time in the legislature for years with the object of maturing and perfecting a general municipal system acceptable to the people and commensurate with their progress in self-government, it is sufficient to say that some time before 1867, when the provinces were confederated, Upper and Lower Canada enjoyed at last local institutions resting on an essentially popular basis, and giving every possible facility for carrying out desirable public improvements in the municipal divisions. The tendency of legislation indeed for years took a dangerous direction. Acts were passed, in 1853 and subsequent years, enabling the municipalities to borrow money for the construction of railways on the guarantee of the province.[2] The result was much extravagance in the public expenditures and the increase of local taxation in many muncipalities of Canada, which hampered the people for many years, notwithstanding the benefits derived from the construction of important public works, until the government was forced to come to their assistance and relieve them of the burdens they had imposed upon themselves.

At the present time, all the provinces of the Dominion of Canada enjoy a system of local self-government which enables the people in every local division, whether it be a village, town, township, parish, city, or county, to manage their own internal affairs in accordance with the liberal provisions of the various statutory enactments which are the result of the wisdom of the various legislatures of the different provinces within half a century. It is in the great province of Ontario that we find the system in its complete form. While this system

---

[1] In 1855 Mr. Drummond, then attorney-general, brought in a bill restoring the parish municipality, while preserving the county organization. Turcotte, ii. 260.

[2] Turcotte, ii. 202. See Consol. Stat. 22 Vict. c. 83.

is quite symmetrical in its arrangement, it is also thoroughly practical, and rests upon the free action of the ratepayers in each municipality. The whole organization comprises:—

(1.) The minor municipal corporations, consisting of townships, being rural districts of an area of eight or ten square miles, with a population of from 3000 to 6000.

(2.) Villages with a population of over 750.

(3.) Towns with a population of over 2,000. Such of these as are comprised within a larger district termed a "county," constitute

(4.) The county municipality, which is under the government of a council composed of the heads of the different minor municipal divisions in such counties as have already been constituted in the province.

(5.) Cities are established from the growth of towns when their population exceeds 15,000,[1] and their municipal jurisdiction is akin to that of counties and towns combined. The functions of each municipality are commensurate with their respective localities.[2]

The Council of every county consists of the Reeves and Deputy Reeves of the townships and villages within the county, and one of the Reeves or Deputy Reeves shall be the Warden. The Council of every city consists of the Mayor, and three Aldermen for every ward. The Council of every town consists of the Mayor and of three Councillors for every ward where there are less than five wards, and of two for each ward where there are five or more wards. The Council of every incorporated village and of every township consists of one Reeve (who presides) and of four Councillors. The

---

[1] As a matter of fact, while the general law provides as above, for many years past it has been the practice for towns in Ontario, when they have a population of ten thousand souls, to obtain a special act of incorporation as a city. See case of City of St. Thomas, Ont., Stat. 44 Vict., c. 46. Also, City of Guelph, 1879.

[2] Canadian Economics; Montreal Meeting of the British Association, 1884, p. 317.

persons elected must be natural-born or naturalized subjects of the Queen, reside within the municipality, and be possessed of a certain legal or equitable freehold or leasehold varying from $400 in townships to $1,500 in cities for freehold, and from $800 to $3,000 for leasehold. The electors must be ratepayers in the municipality. Widows and unmarried women who are in their own right rated for a property or income qualification sufficient to qualify male voters can now vote at municipal elections in this province. Every election must be held in the municipality to which the same relates. The election is by ballot, and complete provision is made for the trial of controverted elections and the prevention of corrupt practices. The municipal officers comprise a Warden, Mayor or Reeve, Clerk, Treasurer, Assessors, Collectors, Auditors, Valuators. The Mayors, Reeves, Aldermen and Councillors are elected by the taxpayers, but the Warden and all the other municipal officers are appointed by the Councils. The powers of these bodies are exercised by by-law,[1] when not otherwise authorized or provided for. Certain by-laws require the assent of the ratepayers. The Councils have the power to pass such laws creating debts and levying rates under certain restrictions set forth in the statute: for the purchase of property; for the appointment of municipal officers; for the aid of agricultural and other societies, manufacturing establishments, road companies, indigent persons and charities; for taking a census; with respect to drainage, the purchase of wet lands, the planting of ornamental trees, driving on roads and bridges, the seizure of bread or other articles of light weight, or short measurement; for the security of wharves and docks and the regulation of harbors; for the laying out and the improvement of cemeteries, the prevention

---

[1] This legal term is an historic link that binds our municipal system to the old English township. In the shires of England where the Danes acquired a firm foothold the township was often called "by"; it had the power of enacting its own "by-laws," or town laws, as municipal corporations have generally to-day."—Fiske's American Political Ideas, p. 46.

of cruelty to animals; for the purchase of property required for the erection of public schools thereon; and providing for the establishment and support of public schools according to law; for the regulation of fences; for the preservation of the public peace and morals; for the licensing of ferries; for the establishment of markets, fire companies, sewerage and drainage; for the aid of railways, by taking stock or granting a loan or bonus to the same.[1] These municipal bodies can be restrained in Ontario, as in other provinces, by the superior Courts when their by-laws are in excess of their powers. The Courts may also compel them to exercise their power in proper cases. The provincial Legislature grants the municipal authorities certain powers, and at the same time commits the proper exercise of those powers to the controlling care of the Courts.[2]

The Council of every municipal district in Ontario has now the power to make such material improvements as are necessary for the convenience and comfort of the people; but, more than that, the whole municipal organization has been satisfactorily adapted to the requirements of a national system of education.[3] On the enterprise and liberality of the municipalities depends the efficiency of the educational system of the province. The wealthy communities are able to erect schoolhouses, which are so many evidences of their deep interest in public education and of the progress of architectural taste in

---

[1] Revised Statutes of Ontario, c. 174.

[2] O'Sullivan's Manual of Government, p. 191.

[3] The Reverend Dr. Ryerson, who devoted his life to founding and developing the Ontario system of Public Instruction, said years ago on this point: "By their constitution, the municipal and school corporations are reflections of the sentiments and feelings of the people within their respective circles of jurisdiction, and their powers are adequate to meet all the economic exigencies of such municipality, whether of schools or roads, of the diffusion of knowledge, or the development of wealth." See a valuable account of the working of the system in one of the official publications of the Ontario Government: "Educational System of Ontario." Edited by Dr. Hodgins, Deputy Minister of Education.

the country. The Legislature has also given power to any incorporated city, town or village to establish free libraries whenever a majority of the taxpayers express themselves in favor of such institutions.[1] In Ontario, as a rule, municipalities have taken advantage of the admirable opportunities which the law gives them of promoting the welfare and happiness of all classes, which are so intimately connected with the education and culture of the people. The city of Toronto, indeed, immediately availed itself of the law providing for free libraries, and has set an example which it is to be hoped will be followed by other communities in Canada. The free library, to quote from an eloquent speech delivered not long since in the city of Birmingham, "is the first fruit of a clear understanding that a great town exists to discharge the same duties to the people of that town which a nation exists to discharge towards the people of that nation."[2]

In all the other provinces the municipal system, if not quite so symmetrical as that of Ontario, is based on the same principles. In the province of Quebec the municipal divisions consist of villages, towns, parishes, or townships and counties. The parish is necessarily recognized in the general law provided for the municipal organization of the

---

[1] Ont. Stat., 45 Vict. c. 22.

[2] A very intelligent writer in the *Nineteenth Century* (August, 1886) gives us an interesting sketch of the remarkable civic development of the great Midland capital. "From main drains to free libraries, from coal gas to the antique, whatever concerns the physical and mental well being of her children, that is the business, the official business, of this renowned city of the Caucus. . . . That the city cares as much for the culture of her people as for the sweeping of her streets is the boast of every Birmingham man, from the Chief Magistrate to the humblest master-craftsman bending over his 'factored' work in his own garret. And lastly, in order that the community might have the freest possible scope for its energies, there came into force in 1884 the Consolidation Act, one of the chief effects of which was the removal of the limit of the public rate for libraries, museums, galleries, and the Art School; and, in a word, the extension of borrowing powers indefinitely." It would be well for Canadians and Americans generally to study the recent history of this enterprising English city.

province. When a canonical parish has been once formed by the proper ecclesiastical authority,[1] it may at any time be erected into a municipality by civil authority. Although the law makes a general provision for the civil erection of a parish, it is also frequently found expedient to avoid the expense of the necessary proceedings by obtaining special powers from the Legislature for erecting and confirming a parish for all civil purposes.[2] The County Council is composed of the Mayors of the several local municipalities of the county in which those officials have been elected. The Councillors elect one of their number to be Mayor of the local municipality, while the Warden is chosen by the County Council. The principal officers are the Secretary-Treasurer, who receives and pays out taxes and other moneys in accordance with law, Auditors, Inspectors of Roads and Bridges, Pound-Keepers, and Valuators. The cities and towns of the province are, however, incorporated by special Acts, and their Mayors as well as Councils are elected by the people.

In the provinces of New Brunswick and Nova Scotia, the people were more laggard in adopting a municipal system than in Upper Canada. Nova Scotia had for years a permissive Act on its statute-book, by which any county might be incorporated when the people made formal application to the Governor-in-Council in the manner provided. It was not, however, until 1879 that an Act[3] was passed providing for the incorporation of the whole province. The County Councils now consist of a Warden and Councillors. The Council elect a Warden from among themselves, a Clerk, Treasurer, Auditors, Assessors, Pound-Keepers and Overseers of Highways. All the powers and authorities previously vested in the Grand Jury and sessions, in special sessions, or in Justices of the Peace, to make by-laws, impose rates or

---

[1] See *supra*, p. 28 note.

[2] For example, Quebec Stat., 45 Vict. c. 41.

[3] Nova Scotia Stat., 42 Vict. c. i.

assessments, and appoint township or county officers, are now exercised by the various municipal Councils in the province. The money annually voted for road and bridge service is now appropriated by the Councils of the municipalities under the inspection of supervisors or commissioners.[1] Cities and towns are incorporated by special Acts, and the Mayors and Wardens are elected by the inhabitants duly qualified by law.[2] In New Brunswick a similar municipal system has been for years in operation.[3]

The little province of Prince Edward Island, however, has never established a complete municipal system; the Legislature is practically the governing body in all matters of local improvement. It passes acts establishing and regulating markets, and making provision for the relief of the poor, for court houses, jails, salaries, fire department, ferries, roads and bridges, and various other services which, in the more advanced provinces, are under the control of local corporations. Every session the House resolves itself into a committee of the whole, to consider all matters relating to the public roads, and to pass resolutions appropriating moneys for this purpose, in conformity with a certain scale arranged for the different townships.[4] Charlottetown and Summerside have special acts of incorporation. Provision, however, was made some years ago for the establishment of certain municipal authorities in towns and villages of the island. Wardens may be elected by the ratepayers of a town or village, to perform certain municipal duties of a very limited character.[5]

---

[1] N. S. Stat., 44 Vict. c. i., and by 45 Vict. c. i. and 46 Vict. c. i.

[2] See Act incorporating town of Sydney, 48 Vict. c. 87. It is not easy to understand why the municipal heads of towns in this province should be called "wardens." A distinction should certainly be made between the warden of the county and the heads of the other municipalities. It is confusing, to say the least.

[3] Revised Statutes of New Brunswick, c. 99.

[4] Assembly Journals, 1884, p. 222.

[5] P. E. I. Stat., 33 Vict. c. 20.

In British Columbia, Manitoba, and the Northwest Territories very liberal provision exists for the establishment of municipal corporations on the basis of those that exist in Ontario.[1]

VII.—Conclusion.

I have attempted in the preceding pages to trace, step by step, the various stages in the development of that system of local self-government which lies at the foundation of the political institutions of the provinces of the Dominion. We have seen that progress in this direction was very slow until the people increased in wealth and political knowledge, and were granted a larger measure of liberty in the administration of provincial affairs. We look in vain during the days of the French Régime for anything approaching those free institutions which are the natural heritage of an Anglo-Saxon people. Under the invigorating inspiration of those political representative institutions, which followed the supremacy of England in Canada, the French Canadians, like all other classes of the population, learned, at last, to appreciate the advantages of being permitted to manage their own local affairs. It is noteworthy, however, that we do not find anything approaching the town system of New England during the early times of British North America. Those primary Assemblies of Massachusetts, which were so many representatives of the folkmoot of early English times,[2] were never reproduced among the people that settled the provinces. Indeed, the conditions under which those countries were peopled were antagonistic to the establishment of the town organizations of New

---

[1] See Brit. Col. Stat., c. 129; Man. Stat., 46 and 47 Vict. c. 1; Ordinances of N. W. T., No. 2, 1885. In the Northwest Territory, the heads of the Councils, outside of cities and towns, are designated "chairmen." Elsewhere these officers are known as "mayors." In Manitoba, the old titles of "reeve" and "mayor" are preserved in the municipalities.

[2] "A New England town meeting is essentially the same thing as the folk-mote." E. A. Freeman, American Institutional History, p. 16.

England. The British government, after its experience of the old Thirteen Colonies, decided to guide the affairs of their remaining possessions with the hand of a gentle despotism, and did not permit the formation of institutions which might weaken the allegiance of the people to the Crown. It was, however, a mistaken idea, as it was clearly pointed out in Lord Durham's Report, to have discouraged the establishment, at an early period, of a municipal system in Canada, which would have educated the people in self-government, and made them more capable of grappling with the difficulties of the representative institutions granted them in 1791. However, the genius of an English race for managing their own affairs rose superior to the influence of a paternal government many thousand miles distant, and won, at last, for the people of Canada, a complete municipal system, which may well be the envy of the British people, who are now endeavoring to extricate themselves from the chaos of local laws, which make local government in the parent state so unintelligible to the ordinary citizen.[1] All sections and peoples of the Dominion are equally favored in this respect. Throwing aside the traditions of a race unfamiliar in early times with the institutions of the Teutonic peoples, the French Canadians have also been brought to a large extent into the van of municipal progress, and enabled to promote many measures of local necessity, which, otherwise, they could not have accomplished.

---

[1] "English local government can only be called a system on the *lucus à non lucendo* principle. There is neither coördination nor subordination among the numerical authorities which regulate our local affairs. Each authority appears to be unacquainted with the existence, or, at least, with the work of the others. 'There is no labyrinth so intricate,' says Mr. Goschen, 'as the chaos of our local laws.' Local government in this country may be fitly described as consisting of a chaos of areas, a chaos of authorities, and a chaos of rates." Chalmers' Local Government in England, p. 15. No wonder then that English statesmen have at last awoke to the necessity of grappling with a problem which Canada herself has in a great measure solved.

In a paper of a strictly historic scope, it would be out of place to dwell at any length on the merits and demerits of the institutions which now prevail throughout the Dominion. It is only necessary to say that we should not conceal from ourselves the fact that there is always danger in a system which hands practically to the few the control of the affairs of the many—which, in a measure, encourages the tendency of the majority to shift responsibility on to others, and, consequently, gives constant opportunities to the corrupt and unscrupulous demagogue to manage the municipal affairs of a community in a manner most detrimental to the public interests. Indifference to municipal affairs on the part of those who should have the greatest stake in their careful, economical management, is an ever present peril under a system like ours. The abstention of the educated and wealthy classes from participation in local affairs, is a growing evil which, in some communities in the United States, has led to gross extravagance, corruption and mismanagement. No doubt, if it were possible to resort to the folkmoot of the old times of our ancestors, or to their best modern exemplar, the township meetings of New England, and permit the people to assemble and consult together on their local affairs, a public advantage would be gained; but, unfortunately, such assemblages seem only possible in primitive times, when population is sparsely diffused, and large cities and towns are the exception.[1] The rapid increase

---

[1] Since the remarks in the text were penned, I have had an opportunity of reading a paper on the Town and City Government of New Haven by C. H. Levermore, Ph. D., in which the impracticability of the old town system of New England under modern conditions is clearly proved. In New Haven, there is a dual system of town and city government. The annual town-meeting, the ancient general court for the town (the folkmoot of all the voters resident in the Republic of New Haven), is still periodically held for the election of town's officers, authorizing and estimating expenditures, and determining the annual town tax for 75,000 people. The author cited says (p. 69):—"This most venerable institution in the community appears to-day in the guise of a gathering of a few citizens, who do the work of as many thousands. Only a few understand the sub-

of population, and the numerous demands of our complex civilization, have forced on us a municipal system which must be representative in its character—which must entrust to a chosen few the management of the affairs of the whole community. The dangers of the system are obvious to all, and should be carefully borne in mind by the intelligent and sagacious leaders and thinkers of every community. Happily, as the peril is apparent, so the remedy is always open to the majority. The security of our local institutions rests on the vigilance of an outspoken press, on the watchfulness of the superior legislative bodies, and on the frequency of elections, during which the people have abundant opportunity of criticising and investigating the administration of municipal affairs. On the whole, then, it would be difficult to devise and mature a system better calculated to develop a spirit of self-reliance and enterprise in a community, or to educate the people in the administration of public affairs. It is not too much to say that the municipal bodies of this country are so many schools where men may gain a valuable experience, which will make them more useful, should they at any time win a place in that larger field of action which the Legislature offers to the ambitious Canadian.

---

jects which are under discussion. But citizens of all parties and of all grades of respectability ignore the town-meeting and school-meeting alike. Not one-seventieth part of the citizens of the town has attended an annual town-meeting; they hardly know when it is held." The proposal to abolish this dual system where it exist in New England, and substitute a simple administration, is now familiar to every one. The old system, in fact, has outlived its usefulness.

APPENDIX.

SUCCESS OF THE MUNICIPAL SYSTEM OF ONTARIO.

The author has had permission to make the following extracts from an interesting letter received by him from the Honorable J. R. Gowan, LL. D., of Barrie, Ontario, who was for over forty years actively engaged in the judicial office, and who, in the course of his useful career, had very much to do with perfecting the flexible system of local government which the province now enjoys:

"I have been familiar with our modern municipal system since it was instituted, and with the exception of the first statute passed in 1841 had something to do with the preparation or criticism of nearly every amending Act up to the time of Mr. John Sandfield Macdonald's administration.

"I was rather opposed to the measure of decentralization—the establishment of Township Councils which did not work at all well at first. Many of the men selected for some time thereafter had neither the education nor the experience to enable them to work advantageously under the law, and as respects County Councils, though the number of members was large, their proceedings were in effect shaped and directed by a very few leading men. All that is changed, and the new generation are, for the most part, trained very fairly in the work of deliberative bodies; first, as school trustees, then in the Town and Township Councils. Above all other things, our excellent school system has diffused the benefits of a sound education and given the new men enlarged views. Without these advantages the municipal institutions of Ontario, with their large powers and the indisposition of men of means to take part in them, would have been ere this a curse to the country. The County Councils are now practically schools in which men are graduated in procedure and debate, and taught something of the art of self-government. It is largely from these bodies that aspirants for the House of Commons and Legislative Assembly come. I can remember that in my own county some eight men of this class have, in the course of years, presented themselves for the former body, and of these five were elected, and that nine men have been returned out of twelve candidates who offered for the local Legislature.

"I take some credit to myself for an effort from the first to inspire the body in my own county with a respect for the position. I endeavored to impress on them my views of the advantages of doing things decently and in order—especially the value of well-defined rules of procedure and the importance of a strict adherence to them, and of being governed in matters not fully defined by the usages of Parliament. Even in the matter of externals the County Council of my county has shown a proper spirit, for some forty years ago the Warden assumed gown and cocked hat while in the chair—a usage kept up by all the officials ever since.

"The result of the establishment of local government in Ontario has exceeded my most sanguine expectations. I have on several occasions listened to debates in the County Council conducted with considerable ability and with as much decorum as one finds in the highest deliberative bodies in the country. The County Council sitting at Barrie is the largest body of the kind in Canada, numbering some sixty Reeves and Deputy Reeves; and the proportion of fair debaters is quite up to that of any Legislature I know of. But the number is now too great; that arises from the rapid increase in the population of many municipalities. As good and perhaps better work might be done with half the number. The time is fast approaching when the number must be limited; but it is difficult to settle the proper basis of representation, so marked is the difference in the populations of the several townships and towns. Taking it all in all, however, municipal government in Ontario is a success; there is nothing elsewhere equal to our system. It has its evils; amongst them, the mode of assessment by officers appointed in and acting for each locality. "Log-rolling" is not unusual when the assessment of the county comes to be equalized. But on the whole, I repeat, the system has turned out well on account of the diffusion of education and the general distribution of property, not to speak of the race of British blood who have developed it. These causes, together with annual elections, have been the great safeguards for the due execution of the large powers conferred on the municipal bodies."

To the foregoing testimony, I may add the following passage from an answer by the same high authority to an address presented to him not long since by the Council of the County of Simcoe, where the municipal system has been worked out in its completest form:

"We can now fairly claim that we possess the most perfect system of municipal government enjoyed by any country, and have proved that an intelligent and educated people may be safely entrusted with the management of important matters demanding local administration—matters that would but retard and embarrass the proceedings of the higher legislative bodies, if indeed they were *there* able to secure the attentions they deserved. In many respects our County stands foremost, and having watched its progress from the primitive condition of a 'new settlement,' I am filled with admiration of the patient industry and intelligent energy that have accomplished so much in a period of forty-one years. You know that at first we had barely passable roadways through the 'woods,' that farming operations were conducted in a very imperfect way, that commerce and manufactures were scarcely in the bud, that the few schools which existed were imperfectly served and ill-regulated, while the municipal system was a recent creation, and moreover that ready submission to the law of the land was *not* universal. Many of you will remember the time when this state of things prevailed, and will know what a contrast presents itself as you now look around you—the whole country accessible by excellent roads, and more than that, netted all over with railroads, agriculture in its various aspects carried on intelligently by an educated farming community, free public schools, with efficient teachers under a uniform system, within easy access of all, the laws everywhere respected and cheerfully obeyed, and last though not least, our municipal system permeating every part with its healthy influences—yes, when you look around you you cannot help feeling that ours is a happy and honorable position, and must bless God every day that your lot is cast in a free country, where there is work for all, and bread for all; where honest labor meets its appropriate reward, and where any deserving man in the community may aspire to the highest place and the largest power for serving his country."

www.ingramcontent.com/pod-product-compliance
Lightning Source LLC
Chambersburg PA
CBHW021533270326
41930CB00008B/1226
9783337188948